BODY

The Infographic Book of Us

Steve Parker & Andrew Baker

INTRODUCTION

PHYSICAL BODY

GENETIC BODY

CHEMICAL BODY

SENSITIVE BODY

COORDINATED BODY

GROWING BODY

THINKING BODY

MEDICAL BODY

GLOSSARY

NOBODY IS JUST ANYBODY.
EVERYBODY IS DEFINITELY SOMEBODY.

The most universal human possession works best when loved and cherished not only by its owner, but by closest family and dearest friends. Who wouldn't want to know absolutely everything about their human body, and even more besides?

Infographics are information and knowledge communicated in graphic form. Shapes and colors predominate over words and literacy. Infographics are instinctive to comprehend and fast to assimilate. They transcend language and easily spring back into the memory. They can be understood by anyone, someone, and, indeed, everyone. They even make statistics fun, data entertaining, and knowledge stick like glue.

So it seemed an excellent idea to combine these two topics, human body and infographics. But how to organize it all? Many body books run through the dozen or so functional systems: bones, muscles, heart and blood, digestion, brain and nerves, and the rest. However, we wanted this book to be different.

Going back to Renaissance times and the birth of modern knowledge, the body was studied in two chief ways. One was anatomy: physical structure, materials, and construction; kickstarted by the momentous *On the Fabric of the Human Body* by Andreas Vesalius in 1543. Anatomy's complementary partner is physiology: chemical workings and functions, introduced as a concept in 1567's *Physiologia* by Jean Fernel. These paired topics still form the basis of modern human biology and medicine—and sections 1 and 2 of this book. A belated latecomer is section 3, the genetic body. This has existed only since the mid-20th century, marked especially by one of the greatest discoveries in all of science—the structure of DNA in 1953 by James Watson and Francis Crick.

The human body learns and experiences through its senses, and all the main sensory modalities are explored in section 4. Its parts—cells, tissues, and organs—are also intensely coordinated and integrated into a unified whole, as explained in section 5. Towering over the whole living organism is its chief command-and-control center, intranet hub, and seat of awareness, perceptions, and consciousness—the brain, described in section 6. So far, all of this is in the adult. Every body has a history. It starts as a pinpoint-sized fertilized egg, which increases billions of times in size and complexity, and section 7 tracks this lifecycle aspect. And when things go wrong, medicine is ready to lend a hand, as described in section 8.

No body book can hope to be comprehensive, but being selective, fascinating, intriguing, surprising, individual, regional, and global can work as stand-ins, especially using this graphic approach. Flowcharts, diagrams, maps, step-by-steps, timelines, symbols, isotypes, icons, pies, and bars are all involved. For the basic material they feed on, we are indebted to those who measure, collate, and analyze such vast amounts of raw data, bare facts, and naked information. Our task has been to find, interpret, and transform, so that readers find something appealing to take away. Hopefully you will be encouraged to understand and appreciate your most treasured possession just that little bit more.

PHYSICAL BODY

MILE-HIGH BODY

A typical human body is a massively complex, ongoing interaction of dozens of organs, consisting of hundreds of tissue subtypes, themselves composed of billions of microscopic cells. One way to visualize this colossal complexity and enormous range of physical sizes is to enlarge the body to, let's say, a convenient one mile in height. This is twice as tall as the world's loftiest skyscraper, at which scale humans themselves appear as mere ants swarming in, out, up, and down—although, see below!

377 ft

Tower Bridge (London)

1,280 ft

Empire State Building

6½

The Eiffel Tower (Paris)

9 ft

SMALLEST BONE

Stirrup bone (stapes); found in the ear

LONGEST BONE

Thigh bone (femur)

¼ in

SMALLEST CELLS

Red blood cell (erythrocyte)

SKIN THICKNESS

Typical skin at 6½ ft thick, which is the average height of a door

DNA

At this scale all DNA in the nucleus of one human cell strung end to end would make up a length of just over 1 mile

1 mile = 1.6 km / 1,600 m

8

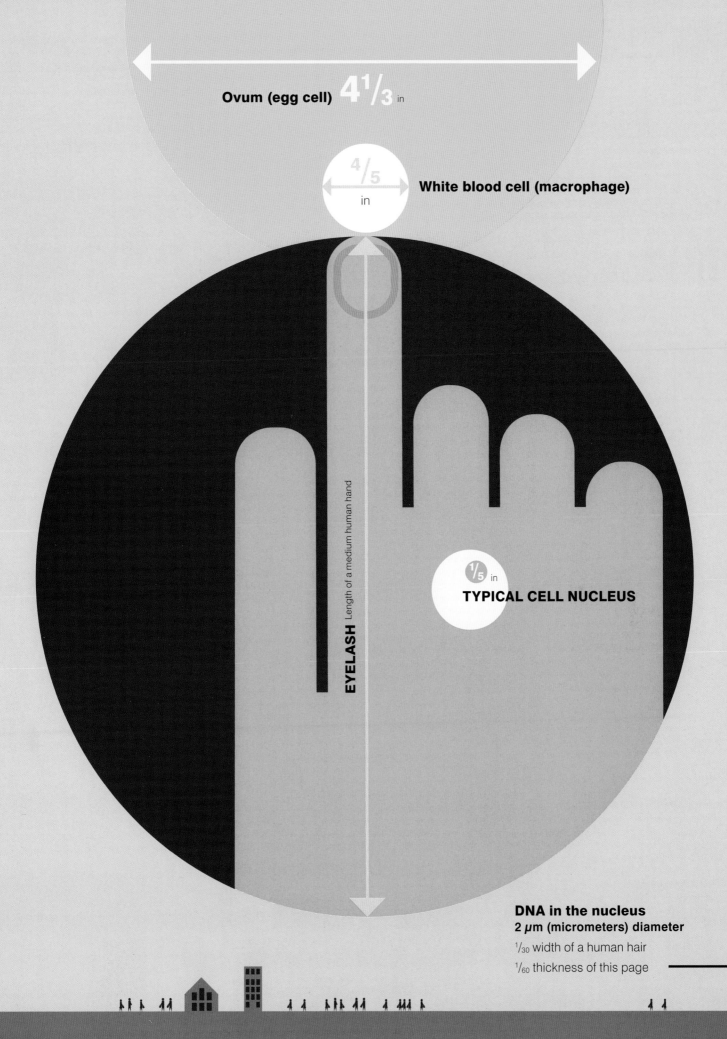

Ovum (egg cell) **4¹/₃** in

4/5 in White blood cell (macrophage)

EYELASH Length of a medium human hand

1/5 in
TYPICAL CELL NUCLEUS

DNA in the nucleus
2 μm (micrometers) diameter

¹/₃₀ width of a human hair

¹/₆₀ thickness of this page

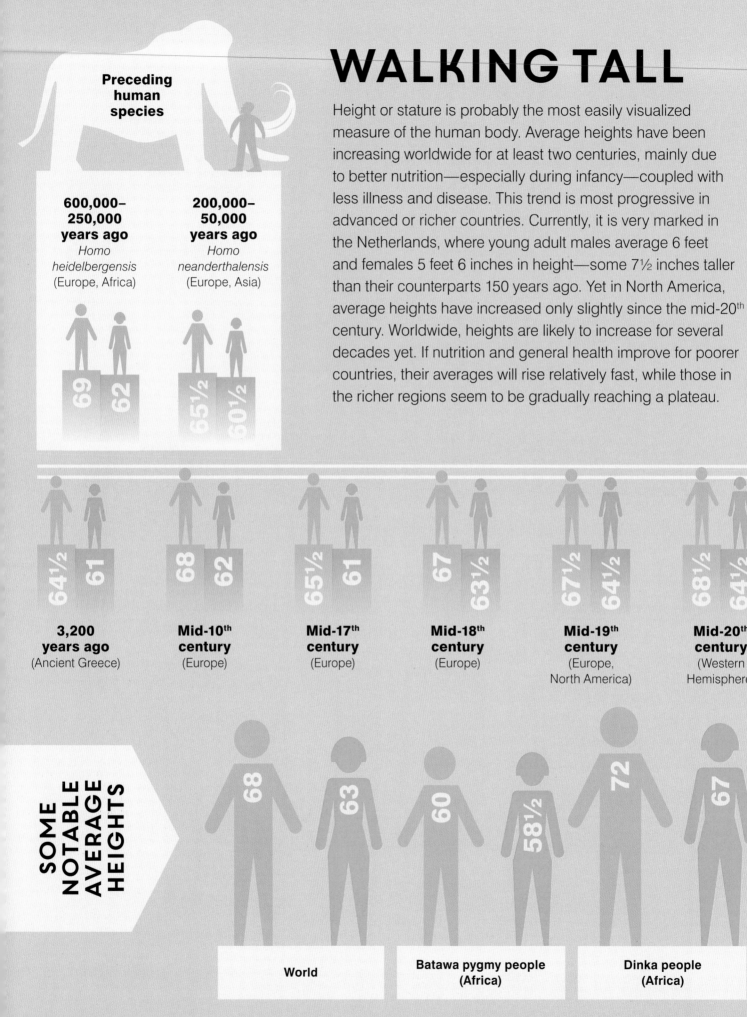

WALKING TALL

Height or stature is probably the most easily visualized measure of the human body. Average heights have been increasing worldwide for at least two centuries, mainly due to better nutrition—especially during infancy—coupled with less illness and disease. This trend is most progressive in advanced or richer countries. Currently, it is very marked in the Netherlands, where young adult males average 6 feet and females 5 feet 6 inches in height—some 7½ inches taller than their counterparts 150 years ago. Yet in North America, average heights have increased only slightly since the mid-20th century. Worldwide, heights are likely to increase for several decades yet. If nutrition and general health improve for poorer countries, their averages will rise relatively fast, while those in the richer regions seem to be gradually reaching a plateau.

Preceding human species

600,000–250,000 years ago
Homo heidelbergensis (Europe, Africa)

69   62

200,000–50,000 years ago
Homo neanderthalensis (Europe, Asia)

65½   60½

3,200 years ago
(Ancient Greece)

64½   61

Mid-10th century
(Europe)

68   62

Mid-17th century
(Europe)

65½   61

Mid-18th century
(Europe)

67   63½

Mid-19th century
(Europe, North America)

67½   64½

Mid-20th century
(Western Hemisphere)

68½   64½

SOME NOTABLE AVERAGE HEIGHTS

68

63

60

58½

72

67

World

Batawa pygmy people (Africa)

Dinka people (Africa)

REGIONAL AVERAGES

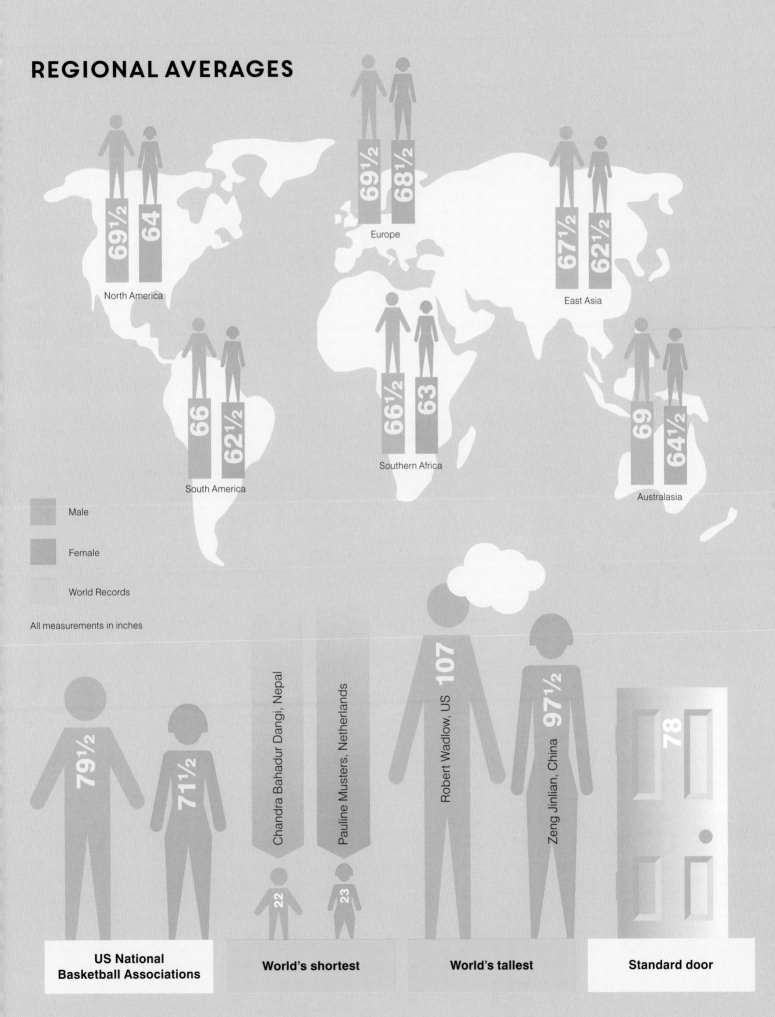

North America
69½   64

Europe
69½   68½

East Asia
67½   62½

South America
66   62½

Southern Africa
66½   63

Australasia
69   64½

Male
Female
World Records

All measurements in inches

US National
Basketball Associations
79½   71½

World's shortest
Chandra Bahadur Dangi, Nepal   22
Pauline Musters, Netherlands   23

World's tallest
Robert Wadlow, US   107
Zeng Jinlian, China   97½

Standard door
78

BODY BUILDS

All human skeletons have 206 bones (apart from rare instances of unusual development or surgical removal). But the relative sizes and shapes of bones vary from one owner to another, giving a variety of basic body builds: big-boned, svelte, long-limbed, chunky, solid, rangy, delicate, and many other metaphorical descriptors.

After growth finishes, the adult skeletal shape determines body measures such as overall height and limb proportions. But the layers that clothe the skeleton also add greatly to the body's general outline. These include several sets of muscles, from deep to superficial, and on top of them, the overcoat of skin, with its endlessly debated underlayer of hypodermal subcutaneous adipose tissue—fat.

Types are independent of height

GENERAL SKELETAL TYPES

1 Ectomorph: Slim, light-boned, "gracile," tendency to leanness

2 Mesomorph: Average

3 Endomorph: Wide, heavy-boned, "robust," tendency to stoutness

Most individuals are combinations of two types.

In the 1940s, US psychologist William Sheldon attempted to correlate body shape and size to personality traits, temperament, intelligence, and emotional states, e.g., ectomorphs being introverted, anxious, shy, and restrained; endomorphs being open, expressive, voluble, and easygoing. This theory has since been discredited.

1,400

HELLO!

hello

WORLD'S HEAVIEST MALE (lb)
Jon Minnoch (US)

Banana

Strawberry

12

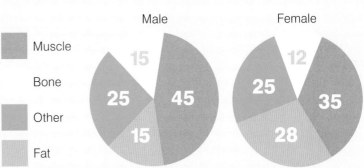

Male   Female

- Muscle
- Bone
- Other
- Fat

Male: 15, 25, 15, 45
Female: 12, 25, 28, 35

1,119

WORLD'S HEAVIEST FEMALE (lb)
Carol Yager (US)

FRUIT'N'NUT BODIES

Fruity or nutty body shapes may be easier to remember than complicated formulae. These portray where extra weight is carried. In general, having abdominal fat (an apple shape) indicates higher health risks than carrying fat around the buttocks and thighs (a pear shape).

Apple   Pear   Peanut

BMI: body mass index

BMI is an approximation designed to relate mass (weight), height, and health implications. It aims to encompass both females and males, and to account for most body shapes, from slim to wide.

Less than 18.5 | 18.5–25 | 25–30 | 30+

M ÷ H² or body's mass (weight) in kilograms divided by body height times itself in meters

WHtR: waist to height ratio

Probably the simplest mathematically for these types of calculations, WHtR is a quick-and-ready indicator of where body fat is distributed.

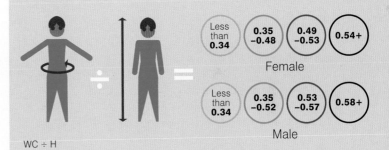

Less than 0.34 | 0.35–0.48 | 0.49–0.53 | 0.54+
Female

Less than 0.34 | 0.35–0.52 | 0.53–0.57 | 0.58+
Male

WC ÷ H

ABSI: a body shape index

A development of BMI, ABSI includes waist circumference (WC). It takes into account body fat distribution and is said to be a more accurate health predicting factor; however, it involves trickier mathematics.

$\div \left(BMI^{2/3} \times \left(\times \right) \right) =$ 0.0808

WC ÷ (BMI²ᐟ³ x H²) or BMI to the power ²/₃ multiplied by body height times itself in meters, divided into waist circumference in meters. The full calculation also includes age and select female/male.

Underweight   Normal   Overweight   Obese

IN PROPORTION

Since antiquity, artists and sculptors have celebrated proportion and harmony in the human form. Of course, bodies come in many shapes and sizes, but much the same proportions and relationships apply to the great majority of them. The well-known golden ratio of 1:1.618 (also variously known as the golden section, golden mean, phi, Φ) is seen extensively in nature and is much used in art to produce lengths and shapes with pleasing and balanced relationships. This ratio also occurs throughout the body.

| 1 | 1.618 |

Head Units ("Face Eighths")
Taking the head/face, from base of chin to crown of scalp, as one-eighth of total body height leads to these typical proportions:

The Golden Body
Golden ratio. For two lines lengths a and b
a:b = (a+b):a = 1.618)

Crown of scalp — 8

Base of chin — 7

Nipples — 6

Navel — 5

Greatest hip width/crotch — 4

Mid thigh — 3

Base of kneecap — 2

Greatest bulge of calf — 1

Crown to neck

Base of neck to navel

Base of neck to navel

Crown of scalp to navel

Navel to base of kneecap

Navel to sole

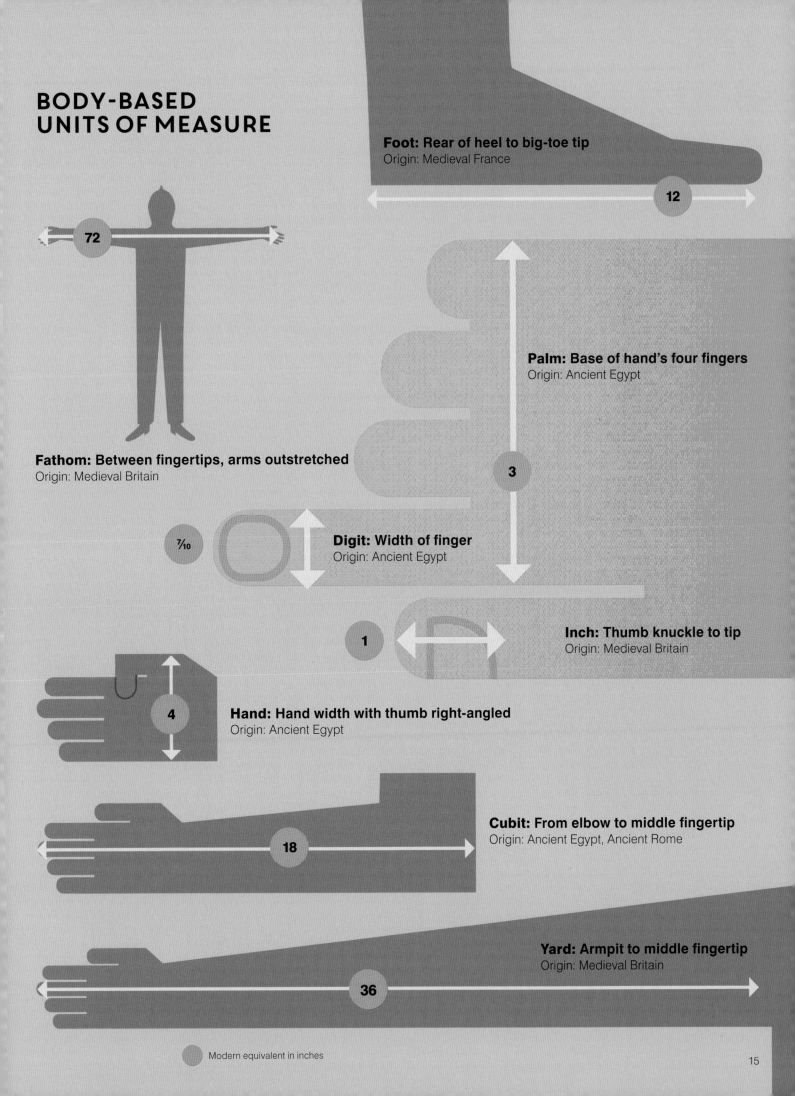

BODY-BASED
UNITS OF MEASURE

Foot: Rear of heel to big-toe tip
Origin: Medieval France

12

72

Palm: Base of hand's four fingers
Origin: Ancient Egypt

3

Fathom: Between fingertips, arms outstretched
Origin: Medieval Britain

⁷⁄₁₀

Digit: Width of finger
Origin: Ancient Egypt

1

Inch: Thumb knuckle to tip
Origin: Medieval Britain

4

Hand: Hand width with thumb right-angled
Origin: Ancient Egypt

18

Cubit: From elbow to middle fingertip
Origin: Ancient Egypt, Ancient Rome

36

Yard: Armpit to middle fingertip
Origin: Medieval Britain

Modern equivalent in inches

SLICED AND DICED

Much as finding a place in the landscape requires latitude, longitude, and altitude, precise location of any part of the body demands a basic set of three-dimensional coordinates, or matrices: up–down, side–side, front–rear. Today's plethora of scanning technologies reveal the body's insides like never before, without a scalpel in sight. These are the "need to know" directions when viewing the body.

TRANSVERSE
horizontally up–down

ANATOMICAL PLANES

SAGITTAL
side to side

CORONAL
front to back

AXES OF ROTATION

LONGITUDINAL
head–toe

FRONTAL
front–back

TRANSVERSE
side–side

DIRECTIONS OF VIEW

INFERIOR
from below

SUPERIOR
from above

LATERAL
profile, away from midline

MEDIAL
profile, toward midline

ANTERIOR
from the front

POSTERIOR
from the rear

DISTAL
extremity toward main body

PROXIMAL
main body toward extremity

SEE-THROUGH BODY

Advanced imaging technologies mean we can see into and even right through the body, and visualize every nook and cranny, without even touching a scalpel. Here are some of the major organs and landmarks that provide good reference points, and which are all explained later in the book.

body coronal section

1 frontal bone
2 orbicularis oculi muscle
3 eye orbit
4 zygomatic muscle
5 nasal cavity
6 carotid artery
7 jugular vein
8 cervical lymph nodes
9 scapula
10 thyroid
11 axillary artery and vein
12 thoracic lymph nodes
13 thymus
14 humerus
15 heart
16 ribs
17 left lung
18 left kidney
19 aorta
20 gall bladder
21 liver
22 radial vein

arm transverse section

1 triceps
2 humerus
3 biceps

head sagittal section

1 occipital lobe
2 cerebral cortex
3 cerebral ventricle
4 corpus callosum
5 fontal lobe

23 ulnar artery
24 stomach
25 radius and ulna
26 carpals
27 metacarpals
28 small intestine
29 colon (large intestine)
30 iliac artery
31 iliac vein
32 appendix

33 inguinal lymph nodes
34 rectum
35 femur
36 patella
37 femoral artery and vein
38 tibia and fibula
39 anterior tibial artery and vein
40 posterior tibial artery and vein
41 tarsals
42 metatarsals

SYSTEMS ANALYSIS

A body system is a group of organs, tissues, and cells dedicated to one (perhaps two) major functions that keep human beings alive and working well.

Integumentary
- Skin • hair • nails • sweat and other exocrine glands

For protection, temperature control, waste removal, and sensation.

Muscular
640 skeletal muscles specialized for contraction.

For bodily movement, movement of internal substances, and protection.

Cardiovascular
- Heart • blood
- blood vessels

For delivery of oxygen and nutrients, collection of carbon dioxide and wastes, temperature control.

Urinary
- Kidneys • ureters
- bladder • urethra

For filtering wastes from blood and controlling overall levels of bodily fluids.

Skeletal
206 bones (usually also including joints)

For support, protection, movement, and production of blood cells.

Respiratory
- Nose • throat • windpipe
- airways • lungs

For absorbtion of oxygen, removal of carbon dioxide, vocalization.

Digestive
- Mouth • teeth • salivary glands • esophagus
- stomach • intestines
- liver • pancreas

For physical and chemical digestion and absorption of nutrients.

Lymphatic
- Lymph nodes • lymphatic vessels • white cells

For draining general body fluids, distributing nutrients, collecting waste, and repairing and defending the body.

Immune
- White blood cells
- spleen • lymph nodes
- other glands

For body defenses against germs and other invaders, cancers, and other diseases.

Sensory
- Eyes • ears • nose • tongue
- skin • inner sensory parts

For information about surroundings (sight, hearing, smell), body position and movement, and internal conditions such as muscle tension, joint position, temperature, etc.

Reproductive
Female: • ovaries • fallopian tubes • uterus • vagina • associated ducts and glands

Male: • testes • penis • associated ducts and glands

For the production of offspring; this is the only system to differ between females and males, and the only system not necessary for survival.

Endocrine
Hormonal (endocrine) glands such as pituitary, thyroid, thymus, adrenals

For production of chemical hormone substances for the communication and coordination for growth, digestion, fluid levels, fear reactions, and many other processes.

Nervous
- Brain • spinal cord • nerves

For collecting and processing information, thoughts, decisions, memories, and emotions, and for controlling muscles and glands.

PARTS MAKE A WHOLE

There are many ways of dividing up a human body. In terms of working roles or functions there are systems, organs, tissues, cells, and their biochemical processes, or physiology. From the anatomical or structural perspective, there are organs and tissues again, the largest being the skin (with its fatty or subcutaneous layer) and liver. Another anatomy-based approach is regional—the head; the torso, comprising the chest or thorax above and the abdomen below; and the limbs, with their various segments.

	BODY MASS %	MASS IN OUNCES IN A 165 lb BODY
Muscles	40	1,058
Skin (all layers)	15	395
Bones	14	370
Liver	2	55
Brain	2	49
Large intestine	1.5	39
Small intestine	1.2	32
Right lung	0.6	16
Left lung	0.5	14
Heart	0.5	12
Spleen	0.18	5
Left kidney	0.18	5
Right kidney	0.17	4½
Pancreas	0.13	3½
Bladder	0.1	2½
Thyroid	0.05	1
Uterus (female)	0.08	2
Prostate (male)	0.03	½
Testis (male)	0.03	½

SIZING THE BODY

Traditional measures for body garments (inches).

Hat
Circumference around widest part (just above eyebrows) divided by 3.15.

Glove
Around the widest part (knuckles).

Collar
Around the fullest part of the neck plus ½ inch.

Sleeve
from center–back of neck to shoulder, then shoulder to wrist bone.

BIGFOOT TREND

Developed regions such as North America and Europe have seen a recent trend to larger feet, especially in women (as shown here by these average adult female sizes). Part of this is accounted for by increased stature—but not all.

US 6½ **UK** 4 **Europe** 37

US 7½ **UK** 5 **Europe** 38

US 8½ **UK** 6.5 **Europe** 39½

1960

1970

2010

Try for comparison!

Shoe
UK shoe-size is based on King Edward II's (1284–1327) foot being size 12 (12 inches), then decreasing or increasing by one barleycorn (⅓ inch) per size.

The human body has

206
bones (usually)

BARE BONES

During early development in the womb, bones form first as shapes of cartilage; gradually, these shapes become ossified, or infiltrated with bone material, and the number of actual bones reaches more than 300 during infancy. Then the total falls again as some of these bony elements, especially those in the skull, join or fuse toward maturation.

Genetic and developmental variations occur, too. About one person in 120 has two extra ribs, making 13 pairs rather than 12. About one in 25 skeletons are "lumbarized," with what appears to be a sixth lumbar vertebra added to the regular five; however, the extra one is a mobile nonfused vertebra "borrowed" from the sacrum below, which has four fused vertebral segments rather than five. Also around one person in 100 has a variant in the numbers of fingers or toes and their bones. Then, sometimes there are the occasional extra bones in the wrist, ankle…

80 AXIAL SKELETON

Composed of four parts
Cranium, face, spinal column, and thorax

31 bones in each leg

32 bones in each arm

DENTAL MATTERS

No part of the body is as hard as the enamel layer covering each tooth. Just under this layer is dentine, also tough and hardwearing. And anchoring each tooth into its socket in the jawbone is the "living glue" of cementum, another robust and resistant material. The whole package—in fact 32 packages, if all adult teeth develop and persist—facilitates almost a lifetime of bites, chews, gnashes, and gnaws, and also grins and smiles.

ADULT TEETH

32:
8 Incisors
4 Canines
8 Premolars
12 Molars

BABY TEETH

20:
8 Incisors
4 Canines
0 Premolars
8 Molars

First incisor	7–8
Second incisor	8–9
Canine	11–12
First premolar	10–11
Second premolar	11–12
First molar	6–7
Second molar	12–13
Third molar	17–21

UPPER TEETH

Eruption times in years

Third molar	17–21
Second molar	11–13
First molar	6–7
Second premolar	11–12
First premolar	10–11
Canine	9–10
Second incisor	7–8
First incisor	6–7

LOWER TEETH

6–10
First incisor (lower jaw)

8–12
First incisor (upper jaw)

9–13
Second incisor

10–15
Second incisor

12–20
First molars

16–25
Canines

24–36
Second molars

Eruption times in months

HOW MANY ROOTS?

1 Incisors, canines, most premolars

2 Upper (maxillary) first premolars, lower (mandibular) molars

3 Upper (maxillary) molars

Wise teeth
Wisdom teeth are the four third molars, one at the rear of each side of each jaw. They usually erupt, if at all, when the individual becomes a "wise" adult, at 17–21 years. But their appearance is variable. They may never really develop, or grow but not erupt, or erupt normally, or grow "sideways" and press into or impact adjacent teeth.

2.5	3	5	5.5	10
Fingernail	copper coin	tooth enamel	steel	diamond

How hard are teeth?
There are many ways of measuring hardness. Prominent is the "rough and ready" Mohs' Scale used for minerals, based on what scratches what, with 10 standards as measures.

LOTS OF LENGTHS

About one-sixth of the body's weight is tubular organs. The blood, lymph, digestive, and urinary systems are basically networks of fluid-containing pipes, tubes, and tubules of diameters varying from greater than that of a thumb to one-tenth of a scalp hair. These various vessels are looped, folded, and coiled with incredible intricacy and intimacy to fit within the human form. But uncoiled and unlooped, and joined end to end, their immense lengths become astonishingly apparent.

DIGESTIVE SYSTEM: mouth + throat + esophagus + stomach + small intestine + ascending colon + transverse colon + descending colon + sigmoid colon + rectum + anus

31 ft

31 ft

URINARY SYSTEM

Nephron tubules (filtering units) in the kidneys.

31 miles

The Grand Canyon

18 miles

Madrid

Paris

TOTAL LENGTH OF

CARDIOVASCULAR SYSTEM

Capillaries	**30,000**
Arterioles and venules	**30,500**
Medium and large arteries and veins	**620**

61,120 miles

2½ TIMES AROUND EARTH!

LYMPHATIC SYSTEM

Average number of lymph nodes for each area:
Abdomen **260**   Neck **150**   Groin **40**   Axillary **40**

400–700

Berlin   Warsaw   Minsk   Moscow

NODES AND LYMPHATIC VESSELS (MILES)

2,485

MUSCLE RECORDS

Extra-oculars
Around sides and rear of eyeball. Rotate and swivel eyeball.

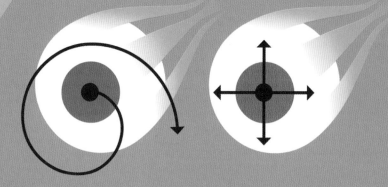

LONGEST

Sartorius
Crosses over front of thigh. Twists and raises thigh.

MEAN MUSCLES

About two-fifths of the body's weight is made up of muscle. There are more than 640 muscles cloaking virtually every part of the body, from the occipitofrontalis found in the forehead to the intrinsic plantar muscles of the sole of the foot.

One characteristic of muscles is their long and complicated names. These may derive from them being on the front (anterior, ventral) or back (posterior, dorsal), and so on, according to anatomical conventions. Or it may be the bone(s) to which they join, and sometimes the nerves they run alongside. Perhaps a nearby major organ. Maybe the motion they effect: flexors bend and extensors straighten. Another option is the muscle's shape: the deltoid in the shoulder is approximately triangular (like a river delta or the Greek letter delta). Indeed, for some unlucky muscles, almost all of these factors contribute to their elongated names.

Up to 23¾ in

BENDIEST

Superior lingualis

Upper surface of tongue (which is actually a complex of 12 muscles). Contributes to the tongue's vast range of movements.

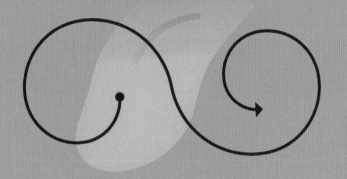

STRONGEST FOR SIZE

Masseter

Side of face and head. Biting and chewing.

LONGEST MUSCLE NAME

levator labii superioris alaeque nasi

| Lifts | the upper lip | and flares the nose's lower side |

It contributes to a sneer and has the easier name of the Elvis muscle, after singer Elvis Presley who made it one of his trademarks.

SMALLEST

Stapedius

Inside inner ear. Dampens vibration from excessive noise.

½₅ in

BULKIEST

Gluteus maximus

Forms most of buttock. Pulls thigh rearward to walk, jump, run.

PULLING POWER

Living muscles are power-packed for their size and weight, but measuring human strength, power, and work capacity is fraught with problems. A single muscle's contraction depends on its basic fitness (especially regular healthy usage or not), the speed of contraction, and numbers of fibers involved (which depends on controlling nerve signals), whether the muscle is already partially contracted or fully relaxed, if it has just been pulling and so may be fatigued, and many other factors.

All together now
It's estimated that if all the body's muscles could contribute to one pulling force, they could lift 20 tons, about three African elephants.

Basic force
A muscle with cross-section area of 1 square centimeter (1½ square inches) exerts a maximum force of 40 newtons—enough to lift a 4-kilogram (9-pound) weight.

SOME COMPARISONS

Power output, W (watt, mouse) or kW (1,000 watts, other) / Power-to-weight ratio, W/lb (watts per pound)

0.2 / 11   **1–1.5** / 7½   **10** / 44   **100** / 132

INSIDE THE INSIDE OF THE INSIDE OF INSIDE A MUSCLE

Muscle, e.g., biceps brachii (upper arm)
Relaxed length: 10 in
Maximum diameter, contracted: 25 sq in

In theory

A fit biceps brachii arm muscle with a maximum cross-section area of 25 square inches could, in theory, raise 570 pounds—equivalent to three or four adults.

600,000 / 1,322,773

600 / 1,984

Fascicles

50–100 mm

5–10 mm

Muscle fibers

5–50 mm

0.01–0.1 mm

Muscle fibrils

1–5 mm

0.001–0.01 mm

Myosin filament

1–3 μm

0.010–0.015 μm

Actin filament

0.005–0.007 μm

0.5–2 μm

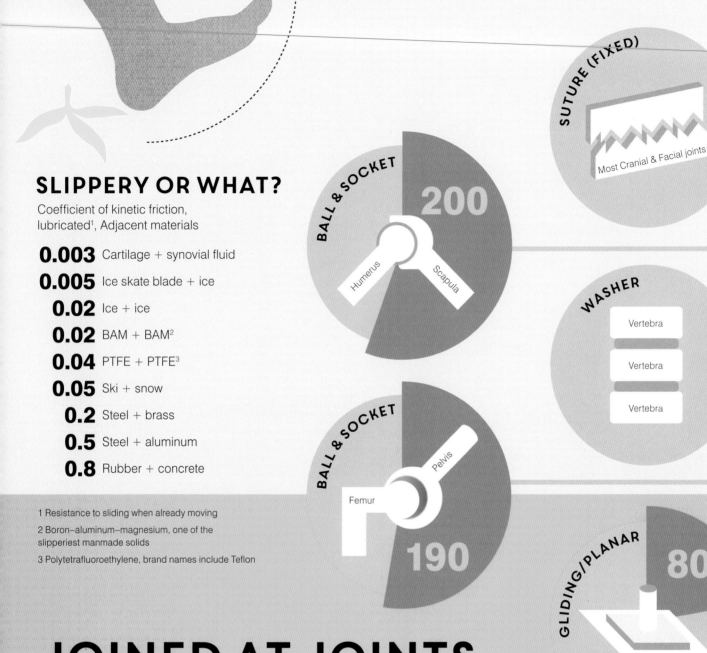

SLIPPERY OR WHAT?

Coefficient of kinetic friction,
lubricated[1], Adjacent materials

0.003 Cartilage + synovial fluid

0.005 Ice skate blade + ice

0.02 Ice + ice

0.02 BAM + BAM[2]

0.04 PTFE + PTFE[3]

0.05 Ski + snow

0.2 Steel + brass

0.5 Steel + aluminum

0.8 Rubber + concrete

1 Resistance to sliding when already moving

2 Boron–aluminum–magnesium, one of the
slipperiest manmade solids

3 Polytetrafluoroethylene, brand names include Teflon

BALL & SOCKET
200
Humerus
Scapula

SUTURE (FIXED)
Most Cranial & Facial joints

WASHER
Vertebra
Vertebra
Vertebra

BALL & SOCKET
Pelvis
Femur
190

GLIDING/PLANAR
80
ANKLE

CONDYLOID
140
TOES

JOINED AT JOINTS

The human skeleton has between 170 and 400 joints, depending on
how they are defined—whether three bones coming together, all in at
least some kind of contact with each other, is one, two, or three joints.
These punishingly physical parts work so well for so long because the
bone ends are covered with slightly soft-cushioned, smooth-gliding
cartilage and lubricated by ultraslick synovial fluid. Also, a tough baglike
capsule encases the joint, and stretchy ligaments link the bones to allow
motion yet prevent dislocation, when bone ends separate—a pain that,
once felt, is seldom forgotten.

Indicates a typical range in degrees for the joint's flexibility in young adults

HINGE

Humerus

Ulna

170

CONDYLOID

140

KNUCKLES

PIVOT

Cervical Vertebrae 1–2

SADDLE

Metacarpal 1

Trapezium

DOUBLE-CONDYLOID

Femur

Tibia

150

GLIDING/PLANAR

170

WRIST

35

BREATH OF LIFE

Take a deep breath. Breathe in a bit more. And more, keep going…
Even the biggest inspiration is unlikely to fill the lungs. The aim of the breathing
process and bodily respiration (as opposed to cellular respiration) is to take fresh
air into the lungs. From here, oxygen passes into the blood stream and on to the next system,
cardiovascular, for bodywide distribution. A secondary goal of respiration is to expel the waste
product carbon dioxide (made by cellular respiration) which, if it rises just 10–20% above normal,
can precipitate gasping, dizziness, even unconsciousness. A third useful effect of breathing is speech
and other vocalizations. So the airways, lungs, and chest muscles keep on breathing, in and out,
around 8–10 million times each year.

810 m

Total air breathed in a lifetime (gallons)

74,000,000

If you sneezed your very hardest, the air speed out of your nose would be 65 ft per second, or 45 miles/h

GASES IN %

78 Nitrogen	
Oxygen **21**	
Others less than **1**	
Carbon dioxide **0.3**	
Water vapor atmospheric (varies)	

400–600
million alveoli (tiny air sacs)

1,550
miles bronchi, bronchiole airways

620
miles capillaries (tiny blood vessels)

BREATHING RATES AT REST

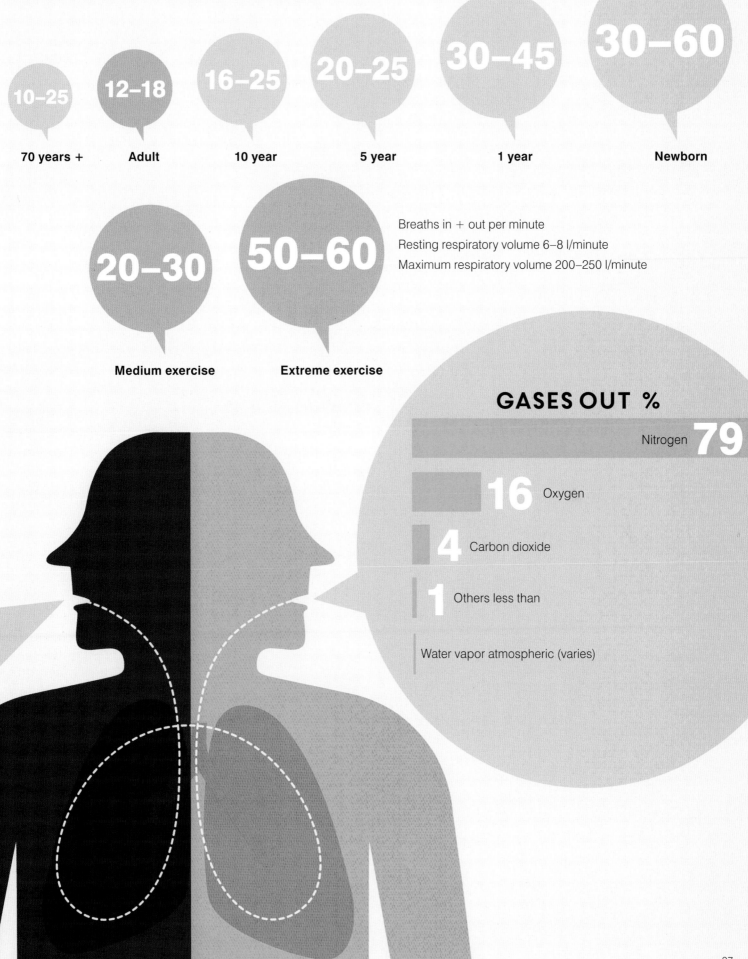

10–25 | 70 years +
12–18 | Adult
16–25 | 10 year
20–25 | 5 year
30–45 | 1 year
30–60 | Newborn

20–30 Medium exercise
50–60 Extreme exercise

Breaths in + out per minute
Resting respiratory volume 6–8 l/minute
Maximum respiratory volume 200–250 l/minute

GASES OUT %

Nitrogen **79**
16 Oxygen
4 Carbon dioxide
1 Others less than
Water vapor atmospheric (varies)

VITAL BEAT

The heart—a seemingly simple double-pumping bag of muscle—beats 3,000 million times or more through a life. When it stops, so does that life (unless critical medical help is at hand). In fact, the heart and its blood system are incredibly complex. The heart itself, even without its body, has an innate or intrinsic contraction rate of 60–100 beats per minute, due to its own set of natural pacemakers. Influences from the body—chiefly signals along the vagus nerve from the brain, and hormones such as adrenaline (epinephrine)—alter this speed, and also the volume and force of each beat, to match the body's immense range of needs.

Heart rates at rest with age (beats/minute)

120
Newborn

90
1 year

80
10 years

60-80
Adult

40-60
Sportsperson

58-80
70+ years

Energy
Each day the heart muscles produce enough motion energy to power a truck for 20 miles.

At rest
A heart would take 30 minutes to fill a bathtub with blood, and an Olympic swimming pool, 5 years.

Carotid
neck

Pulse
A surge of high-pressure blood with each beat spreads out along the arterial vessels.

Felt most easily where an artery is just under the skin and has stiff tissue behind it. Usually at the radial artery in the wrist, just below the thumb mound.

Brachial
inside of elbow

Radial
wrist

Femoral
groin

Popliteal
rear of knee

Dorsal pedal
top of foot

Posterior tibial
ankle

PHYSICAL HEART
Size approximately that of
its owner's clenched fist

12

Average mass in ounces

UNDER PRESSURE

Almost every body part*—every individual cell—relies on flowing blood to bring oxygen and nutrients, and to wash away carbon dioxide and other wastes. Flow is produced by the heartbeat, in two main phases. During diastole ("dye-ass-toll-ee") the organ's muscular walls relax, and it enlarges as blood oozes in at low pressure from the veins—wide, floppy, thin-walled tubes that return blood from the smallest vessels, capillaries, to the heart. Just half a second later comes systole ("siss-toll-ee") when heart muscles tense and contract, forcing blood to rush out away from the heart at high pressure though the thick-walled, muscular arteries, which divide eventually to form capillaries. The pressures involved here are greatest of any body system and make the vessels bulge in traveling waves that spread through their branching network. (*Among the few body parts that do not have a direct blood supply are the eye's cornea and lens; if they did, our world view would be obscured by a reddish mesh.)

THE CAPILLARY NETWORK

Joined end to end
30,000 miles

BLOOD DISTRIBUTION

Approximate % of blood in the body. This means only $1/_{20}$th of blood is actually doing its "real job" of supplying oxygen and nutrients, and collecting carbon dioxide and wastes.

5 Aorta

Heart
5

15
Medium arteries + arterioles

10
Venae cavae

Capillaries
5

60
Venules + medium veins

120/80
mm/Hg
Normal adult

Reasonable healthy range
90–125/
60–85
mm/Hg

BLOOD PRESSURE

Conventionally measured in the brachial artery of the upper arm, by a device called the sphygmomanometer.

Vena cava
(main vein
to heart)

Medium vein

VEINS

**ACTUAL
SIZE**

10

Vena cava

**HOW BLOOD
PRESSURE
FADES**
Internal vessel pressures,
averaged systole/diastole
(mm/Hg)

100

Aorta

Medium vein

15

Venule

20

Capillary

30

Arteriole

60

Medium artery

90

**ACTUAL
SIZE**

Medium artery

ARTERIES

Aorta
(main artery
from heart)

WHAT MAKES A CHAMPION?

The body recipe for a champion athlete is complex, with many different factors at work. They include opportunities to train; the qualities of the coach, nutritionist, physiologist, and other experts; and the equipment, location, and other facilities. A vast amount is in the mind: self-motivation, thorough application, and the will to win; support from family and friends plays an important role here. But perhaps most important is a person's contributing genes: how you are built may equip you better for one sport over another.

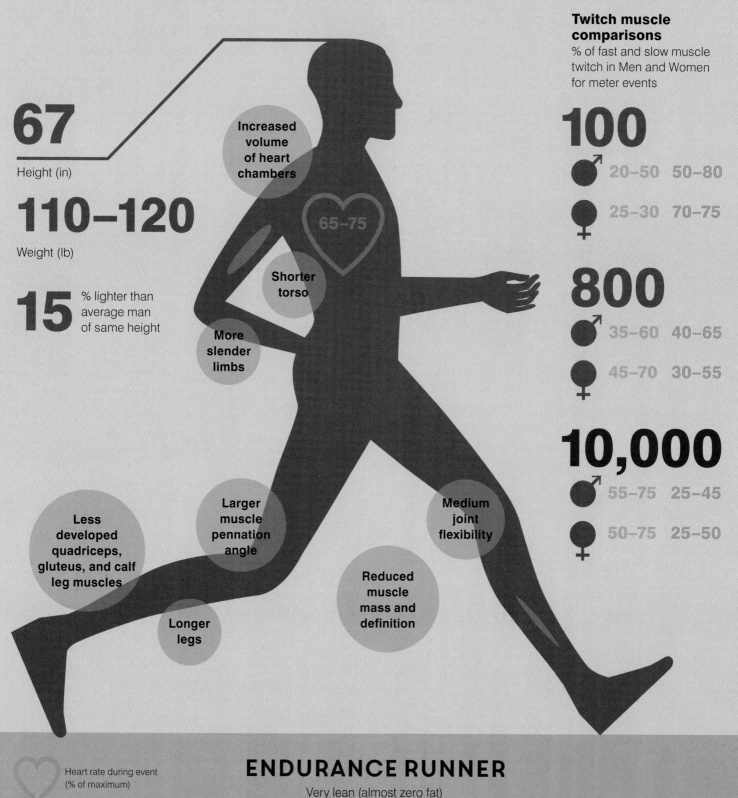

67
Height (in)

110–120
Weight (lb)

15 % lighter than average man of same height

Increased volume of heart chambers

65–75

Shorter torso

More slender limbs

Less developed quadriceps, gluteus, and calf leg muscles

Larger muscle pennation angle

Longer legs

Reduced muscle mass and definition

Medium joint flexibility

Twitch muscle comparisons
% of fast and slow muscle twitch in Men and Women for meter events

100
♂ 20–50 50–80
♀ 25–30 70–75

800
♂ 35–60 40–65
♀ 45–70 30–55

10,000
♂ 55–75 25–45
♀ 50–75 25–50

Heart rate during event (% of maximum)

ENDURANCE RUNNER
Very lean (almost zero fat)

TWITCHY MUSCLES

Most muscles in most people have two kinds of fibers. **Slow twitch** (type I) contract more slowly, generate less force, but can work for longer before fatigue. **Fast twitch** (type II) contract rapidly, generate short bursts of strength or speed, but fatigue quickly. Different kinds of training maximize growth and strength of existing fibers, to change their relative contributions to movements. Less intense exercise promotes slow-twitch fiber development, more intensity encourages fast-twitch fibers. The balance of fast-twitch and slow-twitch fibers is determined by genetics. A "strong" version of the gene ACTN3 enhances the proportion of fast-twitch fibers.

80–90

Thicker heart chamber walls

Average torso proportions

Good joint flexibility

Smaller muscle pennation angle

Average leg and limbs proportions

Longer muscle fibers in leg muscles

Increased muscle mass and definition

72
Height (in)

165–176
Weight (lb)

2–5
% lighter than average man of same height

Slow twitch

Fast twitch

SPRINT RUNNER
Lean (minimal fat)

FASTER, HIGHER, STRONGER

In 1924 *Citius, Altius, Fortius* ("Faster, Higher, Stronger") became the official motto of the modern Olympic Games, which had kicked off in 1896. The saying celebrates how, since first staged in Ancient Greece, the human body's athleticism and other skills are taken to the limit and receive global recognition. The Games' 20-plus sports are a world benchmark for the body's physical powers. Since that time, the body's Olympian triumphs have advanced in speed, height, and strength. Many factors are at work in this, however. There has been steady progress in diet, hygiene, and general health, as well as improvements in specialized skills, training, coaching, and equipment. The late 1930s and early 1940s were interrupted by war. The 1950s–60s saw considerable suspicions about steroid and other drug misuse. And there are occasional quantum shifts in a sport's technique, such as the Fosbury Flop in high jump, introduced in the 1968 Olympics. The Olympics remain the standard by which we measure what the body, taken to the limit, can achieve.

10.8 1900 **10.6** 1924 **10.6** 1928 **12.2** 1928 **11.9** 1932 **10.3** 1948 **11.9** 1948 **10.2** 1960 **11.3** 1960 **9.92** 1988 **10.62** 1988

OLYMPIC 100 METERS
Selected improved times only (seconds)

OLYMPIC HIGH JUMP
Selected improved heights only (meters)

Men

Women

1.90 1.94 1.59 2.03 1.60 1.98 1.68 2.12 1.76 2.24 1.82 2.25 1.85 2.39 2.01 2.06

Women's event introduced

Fosbury Flop technique introduced

1900 1920 1928 1936 1948 1956 1968 1976 1996 2000 2004

44

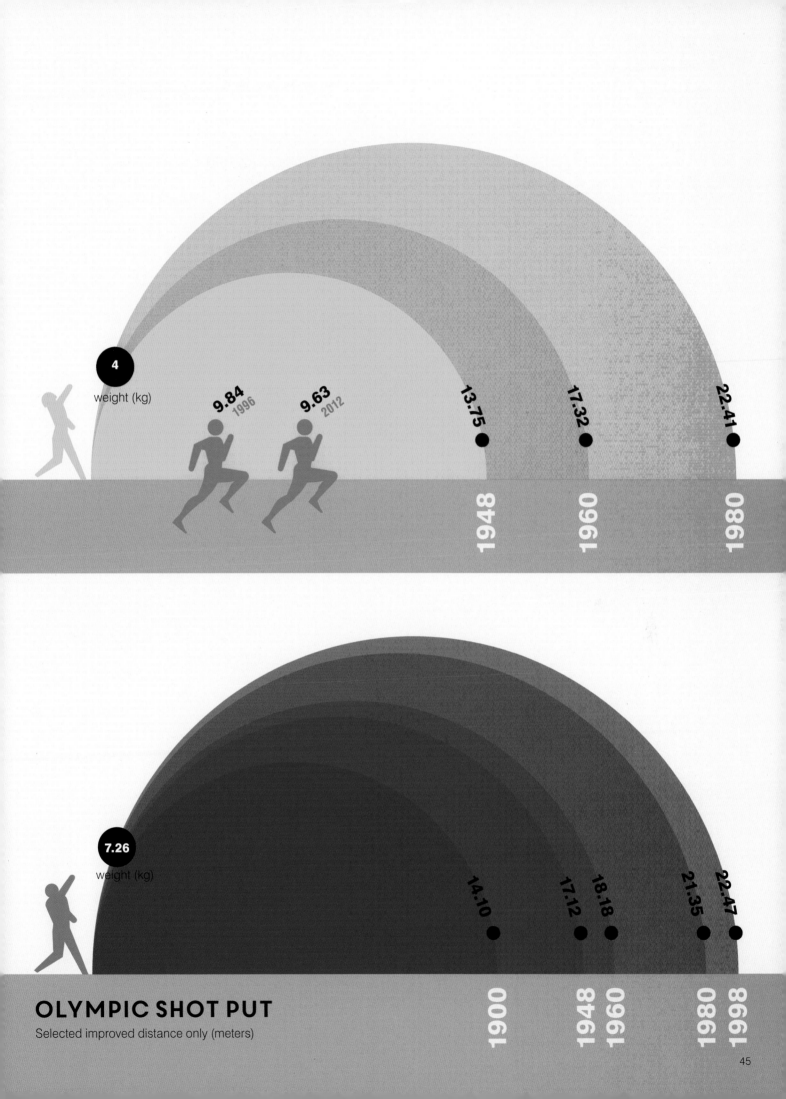

4
weight (kg)

9.84 1996

9.63 2012

13.75 ●

17.32 ●

22.41 ●

1948

1960

1980

7.26
weight (kg)

14.10 ●

17.12 ●

18.18

21.35 ●

22.47 ●

1900

1948

1960

1980

1998

OLYMPIC SHOT PUT
Selected improved distance only (meters)

CHEMICAL BODY

THE CHEMICAL FACTORY

Everything is made of atoms. The human body is no exception and estimates abound as to its proportions of various pure chemical substances. How are these inventories compiled? One way is to list elements by percentage mass (weight); this favours heavier elements such as iron, whose atoms are almost 56 times heavier than those of the lightest element, hydrogen. Another method is to itemize by numbers of atoms; since water (H_2O) makes up 60% of most bodies, this approach promotes its two elements, hydrogen and oxygen. So hydrogen comprises 9–10% of the body by mass, but 65–70% by numbers of atoms.

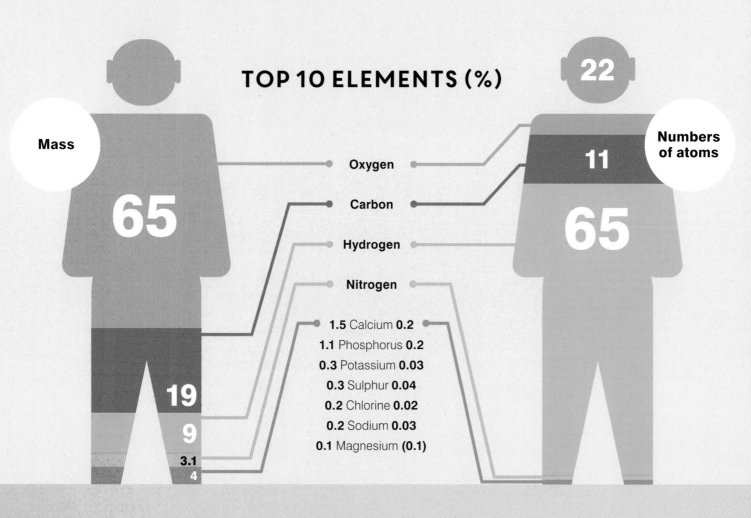

TOP 10 ELEMENTS (%)

Mass

Numbers of atoms

65

22

11

65

19

9

3.1

4

Oxygen

Carbon

Hydrogen

Nitrogen

1.5 Calcium **0.2**
1.1 Phosphorus **0.2**
0.3 Potassium **0.03**
0.3 Sulphur **0.04**
0.2 Chlorine **0.02**
0.2 Sodium **0.03**
0.1 Magnesium **(0.1)**

A 155 LB BODY HAS ENOUGH...

O Oxygen for...

5

large oxygen therapy cylinders (99 lb)

Fe Iron for...

6

steel paperclips (¹⁄₁₀ oz)

N Nitrogen for...

10

sacks of garden compost (4½ lb)

TRACE MINERAL ELEMENTS AT LESS THAN 0.1%

Periodic table with highlighted elements:

Labeled (bold/highlighted): Boron (B), Silicon (Si), Fluorine (F), Vanadium (V), Chromium (Cr), Manganese (Mn), Iron (Fe), Cobalt (Co), Copper (Cu), Zinc (Zn), Selenium (Se), Molybdenum (Mo), Tin (Sn), Iodine (I), Gold (Au)

Row 1: H | | He
Row 2: Li Be | B C N O F Ne
Row 3: Na Mg | Ai Si P S Cl Ar
Row 4: K Ca Sc Ti **V** **Cr** **Mn** **Fe** **Co** Ni **Cu** **Zn** Ga Ge As **Se** Br Kr
Row 5: Rb Sr Y Zr Nb **Mo** Tc Ru Rh Pd Ag Cd In **Sn** Sb Te **I** Xe
Row 6: Cs Ba Hf Ta W Re Os Ir Pt **Au** Hg Ti Pb Bi Po **I** Rn
Row 7: Fr Ra Rf Db Sg Bh Hs Mt Ds Rg Cn Uut Fi Uup Lv Uus Uuo

Lanthanides: La Ce Pr Nd Pm Sm Eu Gd Tb Dy Ho Er Tm Yb Lu
Actinides: Ac Th Pa U Np Pu Am Cm Bk Cf Es Fm Md No Lr

Mineral wealth?
All the elements of one body extracted and sold through global trading markets would fetch around

$4,000

There's gold in them thar' bodies!
A human contains about 0.2 mg of gold, making a cube with 0.2 mm sides.

0.000,2 g

H Hydrogen for…

5,000

helium party balloons (13 lb)

C Carbon for…

10,000

graphite carbon pencil leads (28½ lb)

P Phosphorus for…

20,000

match heads (28 oz)

49

THE WET BODY

Human bodies are mostly water. The broad-spectrum, averaged proportion is two-thirds, which naturally varies according to conditions and circumstances. A higher proportion of body fat, for example, reduces the overall percentage, because fatty tissue contains much less water than other body tissues, including bone. Even so, the body has a lot of water—more than 12 gallons for a 155-pound person, enough for a quick shower. With the water from three bodies, you could wallow in a reasonably large bathtub.

It's not possible to keep the water in the body in the body. Water must leave to carry away dissolved and potentially harmful wastes, chiefly in urine. Around six pints daily generally suffices for this turnover. But it's more in hot conditions, when active, and when imbibing substances such as alcohol.

60 Inside cells (intracellular)

10 Organs (e.g., gut, brain, eye)

10 Blood (chiefly as plasma)

20 Around Cells (interstitial)

% of water not in cells (extracellular)

Where water is found
Biologists talk of "compartments" of water. Not neat chambers inside the body, rather estimated accumulated totals of water in and between and around the millions of cells, hundreds of tissues, and dozens of organs.

Average water (by mass) with age in %

75 Newborn

65 1 year

58–65 Young adult female

65–68 Young adult male

55–60 Middle age

53–55 Senior (70+)

TURNOVER OF WATER PER DAY (fl oz) 90

25	FOOD
10	METABOLIC WATER[1]
55	DRINKS

Water in organs and tissues

By mass in %. Includes their internal fluids, e.g., blood, urine

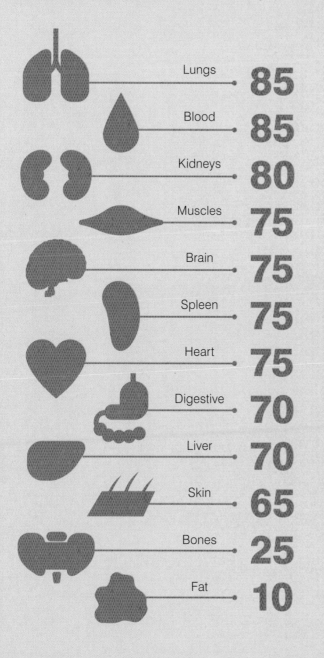

Lungs	**85**
Blood	**85**
Kidneys	**80**
Muscles	**75**
Brain	**75**
Spleen	**75**
Heart	**75**
Digestive	**70**
Liver	**70**
Skin	**65**
Bones	**25**
Fat	**10**

5	FECES
60	URINE
25	SKIN, LUNGS[2]

90

1 When sugars and similar carbohydrates are broken down to release their energy, one natural byproduct of the chemical process is water. This contributes to the body's water income. $C_6H_{12}O_6 + 6CO_2 > 6CO_2 + 6H_2O$ + energy, or, in words, sugar + oxygen > carbon dioxide + water + energy

2 Tiny amounts of water ooze from the skin in almost all conditions, known as "insensible" sweat. Also, the air that is breathed out is almost saturated with water vapor evaporated from the moist linings of the lungs and airways.

MICRONUTRIENTS

The body needs many nutrients in quantities far less than the major macronutrients of carbohydrates, fats, proteins, and dietary fiber. Most "micros" are vitamins and minerals. Vitamins are organic substances that are needed for the body to run smoothly. Most must come readymade in the diet as the human body cannot manufacture them itself in sufficient quantities. Minerals are simple chemical substances, for example, metals such as sodium, iron, calcium, and manganese, and nonmetals or salt-formers such as chloride, fluoride, and iodide.

DAILY INTAKES[1] IN MILLIGRAMS[2]

3,000

Salt

Chloride[3]

900

Eggs

Sulfur[4]

200

Sweet potato

Potassium

800

Pumpkin seeds

Phosphorus

300

Spinach

Magnesium

MAJOR MINERALS

The body requires these major minerals in amounts of at least 100 milligrams (0.1 grams) per day.

2,000

Salt

Sodium

VITAMINS

Most vitamins are required in very small amounts, in some cases a few millionths of a gram.

15
B3 niacin

B5 pantothenic acid **5**

20
E tocopherol

75–90

C ascorbic acid

A retinol group **0.7–0.9**

1.5–1.7 B6 pyridoxine

B2 riboflavin **1–1.3**

1–1.2 B1 thiamin

Relative scale of vitamins in relation to minerals.

90

18

Some vitmains are required in even smaller dosages

400–600 µg[5] B9/Bc/M folate, folic acid
90–120 µg K Phylloquinone, metaquinones
30 µg B7 Biotin
10–15 µg D cholecalciferol
2–2.5 µg B12 cobalamine

18
Iron

Fluoride **4**

TRACE MINERALS

This is a far from complete list, which would continue for several dozen pages of this book.

2 Manganese

2 Copper

Molybdenum ·

15
Zinc

· Iodide

Selenium ·

· Chromium

Milk

1,000
Calcium

1 RDI Reference or Recommended Daily Intake; many similar categories exist such as RDA Recommended Daily Allowance, AI Adequate Intake

2 mg milligrams (0.001 or one-thousandth of a gram) unless stated

3 As sodium chloride (table or common salt)

4 Sulfur has no official RDI; quantities are based on average healthy intake

5 µg micrograms (0.000,001 or one-millionth of a gram; 0.001 or one-thousandth of a milligram)

MACRONUTRIENTS

Recommended macronutrients in grams for a standard daily food intake that supplies energy of 8,700 kJ (kilojules) or 2,100 Calories (kcal).

300–310

Carbohydrates

90

Glucose and other sugars

0.3 Cholesterol

65–70

Total fats

20–25
Saturated
fatty acids

20–25
Dietary fiber

45–55
Total proteins

YOUR ORGANS AND ENERGY (%)

Main energy users for a fairly active individual.

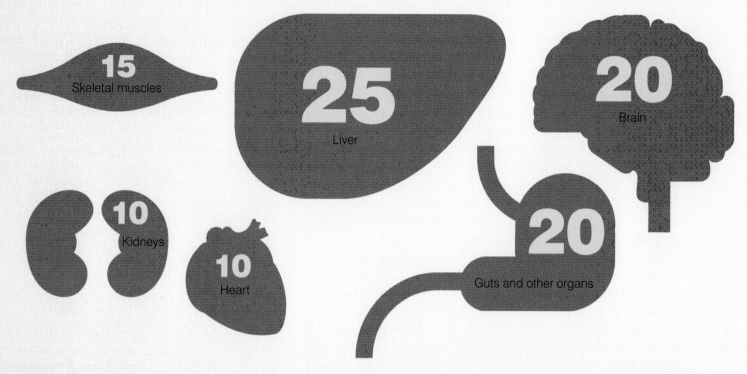

15 Skeletal muscles

25 Liver

20 Brain

10 Kidneys

10 Heart

20 Guts and other organs

MYSTERIES OF METABOLISM

The term "metabolism" is a convenient catch-all shorthand for the immense number of chemical reactions, changes, and processes occurring throughout every cell of the body, every second of every day, many of which are interlinked and interdependent. Estimates of how many individual chemical reactions happen soon run into millions, then billions, then off the chart. However, the body's use of energy for metabolism has been studied intensively and contributes to many areas of knowledge, from mainstream physiology, through sports diets, to designing survival rations for extreme conditions.

ENERGY USE (%)

Use of energy (based on factors such as relatively stress-free environment, ambient body temperature, empty stomach).

15 Heat production

25 Physical activities

60 Basic Metabolic Rate, basic life processes

LIFESTYLES AND ENERGY NEEDS (KJ/DAY)

Work examples

1 Sedentary: mostly desk tasks

2 Lightly active: store staff, nursing, deliveries

3 Very active: construction, gardening/landscaping, semi-professional or professional sports

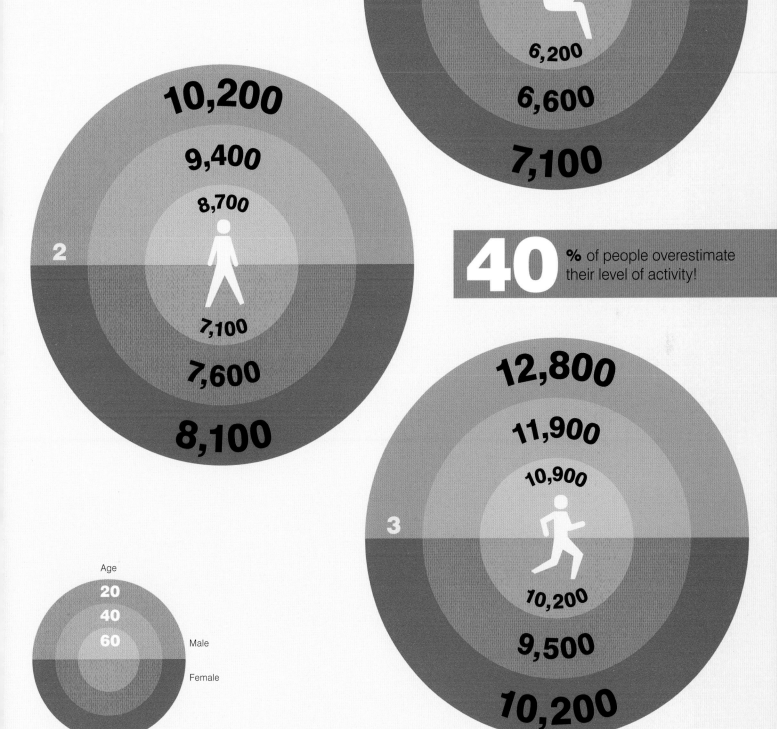

9,000
8,300
7,600
6,200
6,600
7,100

10,200
9,400
8,700
7,100
7,600
8,100

40% of people overestimate their level of activity!

12,800
11,900
10,900
10,200
9,500
10,200

Age
20
40
60
Male
Female

INS AND OUTS OF ENERGY

The body is an energy transformer. It takes in chemical energy, in the form of trillions of bonds between atoms and molecules in foods and drinks. By the myriad processes of metabolism it converts this energy into other forms, especially the kinetic energy of movement, the thermal energy of heat, the electrical energy of nerve signals, and miscellaneous types such as the sound energy of speech.

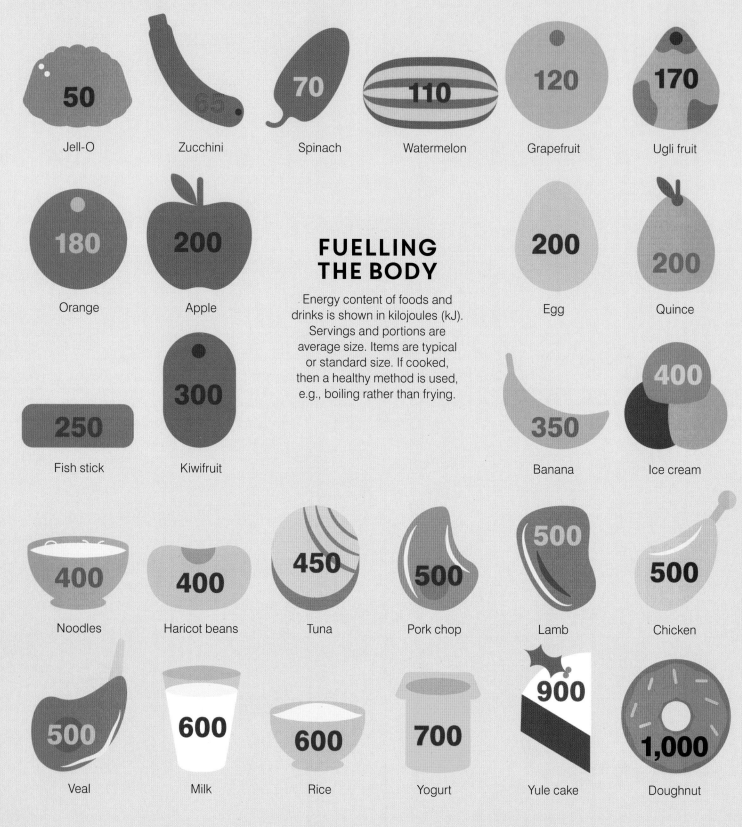

50 Jell-O

65 Zucchini

70 Spinach

110 Watermelon

120 Grapefruit

170 Ugli fruit

180 Orange

200 Apple

200 Egg

200 Quince

250 Fish stick

300 Kiwifruit

350 Banana

400 Ice cream

FUELLING THE BODY

Energy content of foods and drinks is shown in kilojoules (kJ). Servings and portions are average size. Items are typical or standard size. If cooked, then a healthy method is used, e.g., boiling rather than frying.

400 Noodles

400 Haricot beans

450 Tuna

500 Pork chop

500 Lamb

500 Chicken

500 Veal

600 Milk

600 Rice

700 Yogurt

900 Yule cake

1,000 Doughnut

Over time, too much energy coming in and not then used is eventually converted into body fat. And energy use varies depending on: body mass—heavier bodies use more; gender—females use typically 5–10% less than males; and age—expenditure decreases with increasing years. In a typical body, two pounds of body fat contains enough energy to run between three and four marathons.

2–15

Asleep

3–6

Awake, inactive

8

Ironing

10

Yoga

14

Walk 2½ mph

15

Slow ballroom dance

15

Vacuuming

18

Light aerobics

ENERGY USE IN VARIOUS ACTIVITIES

Sports played at local competitive club level. Examples based on a male body mass of 143–165 lb.

Units are kJ/min or kilojoules per minute

1kJ = 0.24 Calories/kilocalories

1 Calorie = 4.18 kJ

18

Cycling 6 mph

20

Fast ballroom dance

20

Climbing stairs, slow

23

Swim 27 yards/min

25

Walk 4 mph

35

Vigorous aerobics

40

Soccer

41

Cycling 12 mph

42

Run 5 mph

45

Climbing stairs, fast

49

Run 6 mph

50

Tennis

54

Swim 55 yards/min

55

Squash

66

Run 9 mph

200+

Run full speed

DISASSEMBLY LINE

Apart from breathed-in oxygen, every last bit of the human body's energy comes from its food and drink. Acquiring these substances is the task of digestion, and it's an epic story of breakdown and destruction. Every delicious mouthful is chewed to a pulp, slides quickly down the gullet, and is welcomed into a stomach bath of strong acid and destructive juices called enzymes. Now an oozing mush known as chyme, the food is further disassembled by more enzymes in the small intestine, reducing it to molecules miniscule enough to absorb through the intestinal lining into the blood. Next is the large intestine, whose task is to absorb water, some vitamins, and other incidentals, before the results come to rest in the rectum, ready for removal.

DIGESTIVE AREA

Most absorption of nutrients takes place in the small intestine. It has features that successively increase its inner surface area, compared to a simple tube (shown here in area, sq ft).

simple 23-foot tube
1–1½ in

6½ ■ 32

Plicae
folds in inner lining

Villi
fingerlike projections on plicae

108

Microvilli
micro-versions of villi

540

2–3 Saliva

3–6 Stomach

2–4 Small intestine

3–5 Pancreas

2 Liver (bile)

½–1 Large intestine

½ Approximately 95% reabsorption means very little water is lost in stools

Digestive juices produced per day (pints)

Digestion involves the production of large quantities of water-based juices, followed by remarkable reabsorption of water in the large intestine. This saves us from having to drink more than 20 pints daily!

1 Assumes healthy, thorough chewing
2 The stomach takes an hour or two longer to tackle fatty foods, compared to carbohydrates and proteins

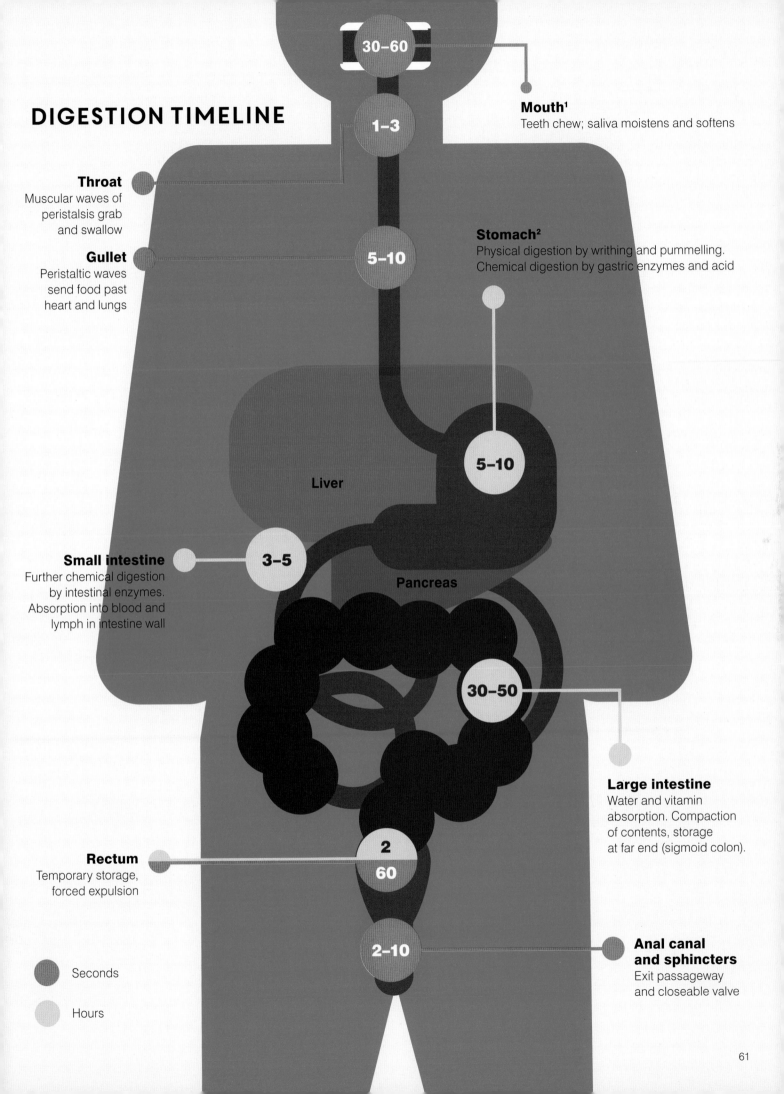

DIGESTION TIMELINE

30–60

1–3

Mouth[1]
Teeth chew; saliva moistens and softens

Throat
Muscular waves of peristalsis grab and swallow

Gullet
Peristaltic waves send food past heart and lungs

5–10

Stomach[2]
Physical digestion by writhing and pummelling. Chemical digestion by gastric enzymes and acid

5–10

Liver

Pancreas

Small intestine
Further chemical digestion by intestinal enzymes. Absorption into blood and lymph in intestine wall

3–5

30–50

Large intestine
Water and vitamin absorption. Compaction of contents, storage at far end (sigmoid colon).

Rectum
Temporary storage, forced expulsion

2
60

2–10

Anal canal and sphincters
Exit passageway and closeable valve

Seconds

Hours

61

BLOOD CONTENTS

About half of blood is water. The rest is the most vital substances needed for life including dissolved oxygen, energy-rich sugars and fats, antibody proteins to fight disease, and vital nutrients, minerals, and vitamins. Delving deep among the red and white cells, numbers and turnover soon become extraordinary. New red blood cells are made at the rate of two to three million every second; each of these cells contains 280 million molecules of the red oxygen-carrier hemoglobin; each hemoglobin has more than 7,000 atoms. That adds up to assembling six million billion atoms per second.

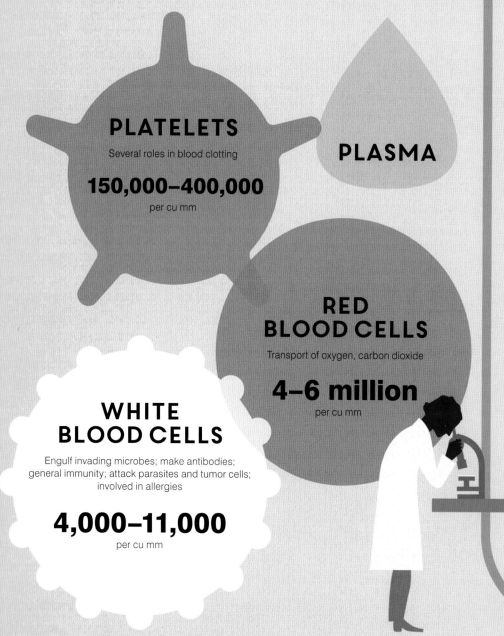

PLATELETS

Several roles in blood clotting

150,000–400,000
per cu mm

PLASMA

RED BLOOD CELLS

Transport of oxygen, carbon dioxide

4–6 million
per cu mm

WHITE BLOOD CELLS

Engulf invading microbes; make antibodies; general immunity; attack parasites and tumor cells; involved in allergies

4,000–11,000
per cu mm

1   0.5

53–57

43–46

MAIN FRACTIONS OF BLOOD

"Fractions" in the sense of relative components or proportions.

Average %

150,000 REVOLUTIONS PER MINUTE

Old-time physicians examined blood by putting it into a test-tube and allowing Earth's natural gravity to separate the components, heaviest at the bottom. Today, fast-spinning ultracentrifuges whirl around blood at more than 150,000 revolutions per minute—2,500 times per second—producing forces of 2 Mg, two million times normal gravity. This separates blood's tiniest components including viruses, DNA, and proteins. Waiting for Earth's gravity to do this would take longer than the predicted age of the Universe.

Below 95
Hypothermia

97.7–99.5
Normal body temperature

Above 99.5–101¹
Hyperthermia

X   °F

THE CHEMISTRY OF SURVIVAL

Temperature is a critical factor in the speed of chemical reactions. The body's immense arrays of biochemical activity—its metabolism—are all finely tuned to happen within a very narrow temperature range. This is usually quoted as 97.7 to 99.5°F, with a common variation of up to 34°F over each 24-hour period. Outside this range, the enzymes that control much of the action begin to lose their effects, and soon one disturbed metabolic pathway disrupts another, with rapidly knocking-on results.

DAILY TEMPERATURE VARIATION (°F)

For a typical daytime routine, core body temperature normally rises and falls through each 24 hours in a natural biorhythm.
Overlaid on this the core temperature also varies by as much as 33°F, depending on surroundings and the body's level of activities.

98.6	97.5	97.5	98.2	99.5	99.3	99.1	99.3
AM	AM	AM	AM	Noon	PM	PM	PM

IN COLD WATER

Depending on water's flow speed, it takes away body heat 25 faster than air. These are approximate times for an averagely competent adult swimmer dressed in ordinary shirt and pants with a collar-style flotation aid.

	minutes	minutes	minutes	minutes	hours	hours	hours
Exhaustion	0–15	15–30	30–45	45–90	2–5	2–10	5–15
Water temperature °F	32	32–41	41–50	50–59	59–68	68–77	77–86
	minutes	minutes	minutes	hours	hours	hours	hours
Probable death	15–30	15–45	30–60	1–3	3–7	3–12+	24+

1 Depends on the normal variation of body temperature through the day and night (see above).

PROGRESSION OF HYPOTHERMIA

Deep hypothermia can lead to two strange behaviours:

MILD

90–95 °F

Pale skin, feeling cold, tired, hungry, perhaps nauseous, shivering, movement problems, slowing down, poor coordination

Breathing and heart rates slow down

? Slurred speech, feeling disoriented or confused

MODERATE

82–90 °F

SEVERE
Below
82 °F

Motor nerves instruct blood vessels to widen (vasodilation)

Skin and peripheral temperature sensors register excess heat due to warmer blood diverted from core

Brain receives sensations of body becoming too hot

LOSS OF CONSCIOUSNESS

TERMINAL BURROWING
Crawls or climbs into enclosed space; possibly linked to primitive hibernation instinct

Brain registers feelings of vulnerability due to nakedness

PARADOXICAL UNDRESSING
Removes clothing

GENETIC BODY

NUCLEUS
Contains genetic material, DNA, that controls many of the cell's activities

NUCLEOLUS
Assembly site for ribosomes

INSIDE A CELL

A "typical" body cell is shaped like a vague blob about 20 μm across, which means 50 in a row span one millimeter. However, there is a snag: the "typical" body cell does not really exist. Perhaps nearest is the hepatocyte or liver cell, which is a good all-rounder approximately as shown here. Most other cells have very specialized shapes and contents, detailed on the following pages. Just as the body is made of main parts called organs, a cell contains organelles. The largest is usually the nucleus or control center, which houses the genetic material, DNA. The other main organelles are also shown here, with their main functions.

GOLGI APPARATUS/ GOLGI COMPLEX
Processes and packages lipids and proteins for use in the cell or export

HOW MANY?

Estimates for the number of cells in the body have **ranged from a few billion to 200,000 trillion (200,000,000,000,000,000)**.

Estimates using cell volume give **15 trillion**, and weight, **70 trillion**.

A recent calculation takes into account cell sizes, numbers, and how they are packed in different tissues. This estimate gives **37 trillion cells (37,000,000,000,000)**.

Counting them at one per second would take slightly more than **one million years**.

CELL MEMBRANE
Controls what enters and leaves the cell and protects the interior

HOW HEAVY?

The typical weight for a cell is 1 nanogram

Which is one billionth of a gram or...

0.000,000,001
grams

CYTOPLASM
Provides the cytoskeleton for the cell's shape, internal framework, and organization; contains dissolved substances.

MITOCHONDRION
Breaks apart high-energy substances, for example sugars, to provide the cell's energy

LYSOSOME
Breakdown and recycling area for old, unwanted substances

ENDOPLASMIC RETICULUM
Synthesis of lipids, protein processing, enzyme storage, detoxification

HOW BIG?

The average size or volume for a human or other mammal cell is

0.000,004
cubic mm

Which is 4 billionths of a cubic cm.

RIBOSOME
Protein synthesis—joins amino-acid subunits to make larger molecules and proteins (see page 76)

CELLS GALORE

There are more than 200 different kinds of cells in the body. Each is specially shaped, and has its own complement of parts and organelles inside, to fulfill its particular role. For example, a nerve cell or neuron has long, snaking projections—the axon (fiber) and dendrites—to communicate with its fellows. Muscle cells are packed with mitochondria as they require plentiful energy, while red blood cells are lilttle more than bags of oxygen-transporting hemoglobin. The examples below list some of their unique characteristics.

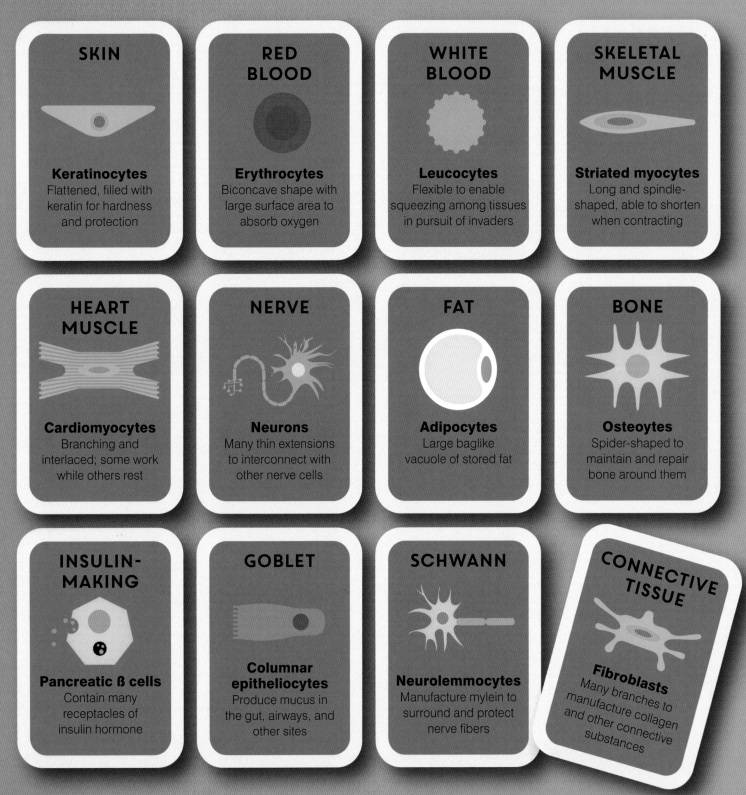

SKIN

Keratinocytes
Flattened, filled with keratin for hardness and protection

RED BLOOD

Erythrocytes
Biconcave shape with large surface area to absorb oxygen

WHITE BLOOD

Leucocytes
Flexible to enable squeezing among tissues in pursuit of invaders

SKELETAL MUSCLE

Striated myocytes
Long and spindle-shaped, able to shorten when contracting

HEART MUSCLE

Cardiomyocytes
Branching and interlaced; some work while others rest

NERVE

Neurons
Many thin extensions to interconnect with other nerve cells

FAT

Adipocytes
Large baglike vacuole of stored fat

BONE

Osteoytes
Spider-shaped to maintain and repair bone around them

INSULIN-MAKING

Pancreatic ß cells
Contain many receptacles of insulin hormone

GOBLET

Columnar epitheliocytes
Produce mucus in the gut, airwygen, and other sites

SCHWANN

Neurolemmocytes
Manufacture mylein to surround and protect nerve fibers

CONNECTIVE TISSUE

Fibroblasts
Many branches to manufacture collagen and other connective substances

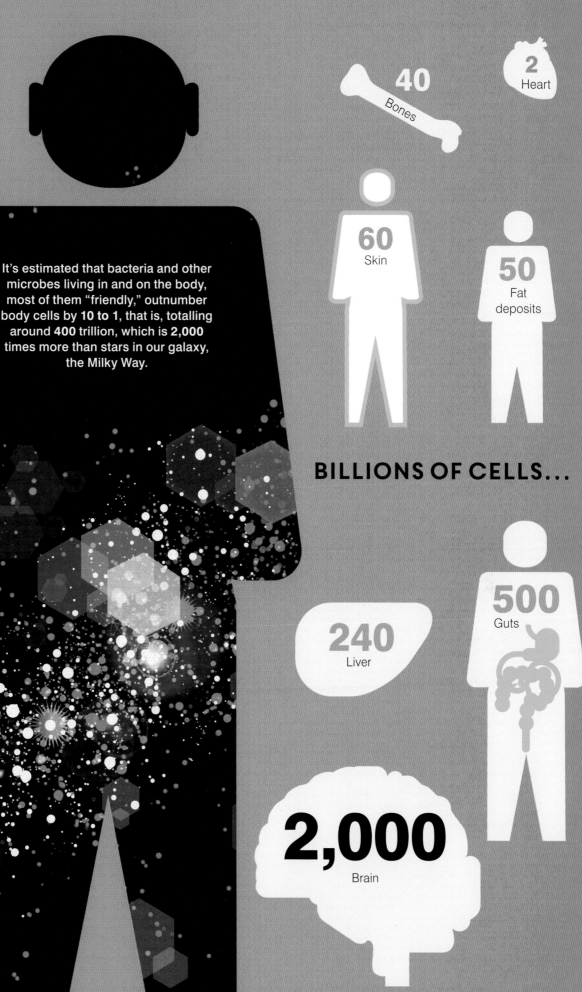

It's estimated that bacteria and other microbes living in and on the body, most of them "friendly," outnumber body cells by **10 to 1**, that is, totalling around **400** trillion, which is **2,000** times more than stars in our galaxy, the Milky Way.

40
Bones

2
Heart

60
Skin

50
Fat deposits

BILLIONS OF CELLS...

240
Liver

500
Guts

2,000
Brain

DOWN AMONG THE DNA

Within the nucleus, or control center, of a human cell reside 46 lengths of the genetic substance DNA, or, to give it its full name, deoxyribonucleic acid. Each DNA length, plus its associated protein substances, called histones, is known as a chromosome. These chromosomes occur in 23 pairs, with the two members of the pair being approximate copies of each other. These lengths of DNA carry, in the form of a chemical code, the genes—instructions for how the body and all its parts develop, work, maintain, and repair themselves.

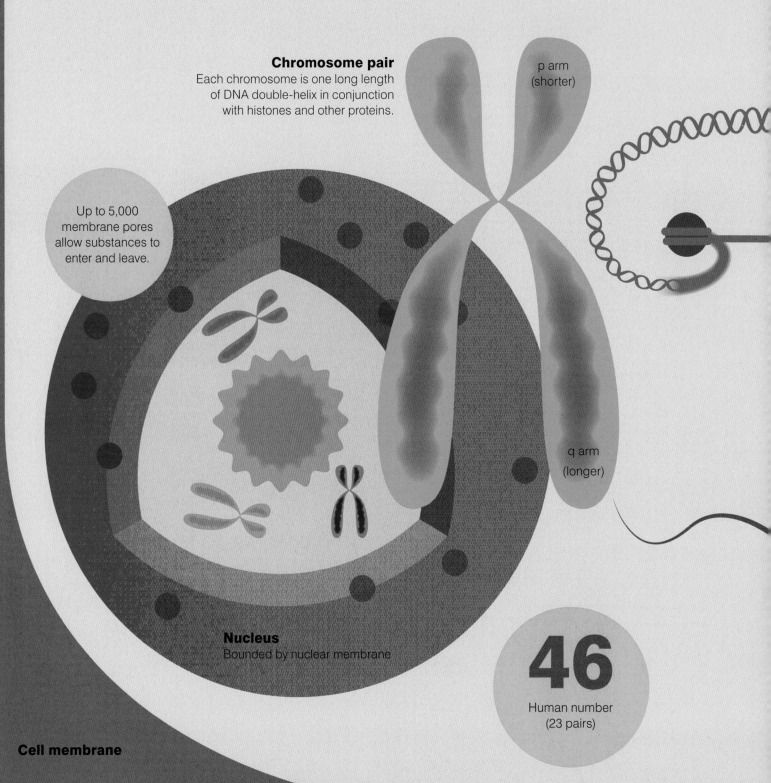

Chromosome pair
Each chromosome is one long length of DNA double-helix in conjunction with histones and other proteins.

p arm
(shorter)

Up to 5,000 membrane pores allow substances to enter and leave.

q arm
(longer)

Nucleus
Bounded by nuclear membrane

Cell membrane

46
Human number
(23 pairs)

THYMINE **A**DENINE

GUANINE **C**YTOSINE

Base pairs
Nucleobases or nitrogenous bases are "letters" for genetic instructions. They are always found in these pairs.

DNA DOUBLE HELIX

1: Wider major groove

2: About 10 base pairs per turn of helix

3: Narrower minor groove

4: Deoxyribose (sugar) and phosphate backbone

5: Cross-links of base pairs

Histone core

Supercoiled DNA

Supercoiled DNA
Supercoiling is a DNA helix wound or coiled on itself.

Nucleosome
One "bead" on the "necklace" of DNA

1.7 supercoiled turns of DNA around a core of 8 histone protein molecules

1   **X**2000 → **85**

2   **X**1400 → **83**

3   **X**1000 → **67**

4   **X**1000 → **65**

6   **X**1000   **58**

7   **X**900   **54**

8   **X**700   **50**

9   **X**800   **48**

14   **X**800   **36**

15   **X**600   **35**

16   **X**800   **31**

17   **X**1200   **28**

22   **X**500 → **17**

X 23   **X**800   **53**

Y ♂   **X**50 **20**

X   Estimated number of genes in the chromosome

ACTUAL LENGTH   Length (mm) of the DNA in each chromosome when unraveled

KARYOTYPE

A karyotype is the appearance of all the chromosomes in a particular organism, usually laid out in a row. In the human karyotype there are:

22 pairs
of identical-looking chromosomes, numbered approximately in order of decreasing size.

The 23rd pair are dissimilar and known as **X** and **Y** sex chromosomes.

5

X900 ← **62**

10 — **X700** ← **46**

11 — **X1300** ← **46**

12 — **X1100** **45** ←

13 — **X300** **39** ↓

18 — **X200** → **27**

19 — **X1500** → **20**

20 — **X500** → **21**

21 — **X200** **16**

THE GENOME

The full set of genetic instructions for the body is known as the human genome. It is carried in the cell nucleus by 46 strands of DNA double-helix, each one immensely long in molecular terms, but far too thin to see under a light microscope. However, as the cell prepares to divide, each snaking DNA length twines and twists onto itself into supercoils and supersupercoils. Eventually it takes up a shorter, thicker, condensed, X-like form that, with a suitable stain (dye), is visible under the microscope. These items became known as chromosomes, "colored bodies"—a term that applies whether they are in condensed X-shapes ready for cell division (in duplicated pairs shown here), or strung out and meandering as they dispense instructions.

HOW GENES WORK

Genes are directions for how the body develops and works. But what do they actually do? Like a blueprint plan or instruction book, a gene is a length of DNA that holds the information, as a chemical code, to build a part of the body. This part is usually molecular in scale. For many genes, the parts are proteins, such as actin and myosin, which power muscles; collagen and keratin that toughen skin; amylase and lipase and other digestive enzymes, and hundreds of others. Further genes direct the construction of different kinds of RNAs, ribonucleic acids, which are heavily involved in organizing and running the cell's activities— including control of its genes.

FIRST STAGE: TRANSCRIPTION INSIDE THE NUCLEUS

RNA differs from DNA in one base, it does not have thymine but has uracil instead.

Chemical code of DNA copies to mRNA (messenger RNA)

1 DNA unzips along base pairs, leaving free bases that constitute a gene

2 Length of mRNA is constructed by RNA polymerase enzyme

3 Completed mRNA has complementary base-pair coding to DNA, which carries the genetic information

4 mRNA moves out of nucleus into cytoplasm

5 Ribosome (made of rRNA, ribosomal RNA) moves along mRNA and reads each set of three bases, called a codon

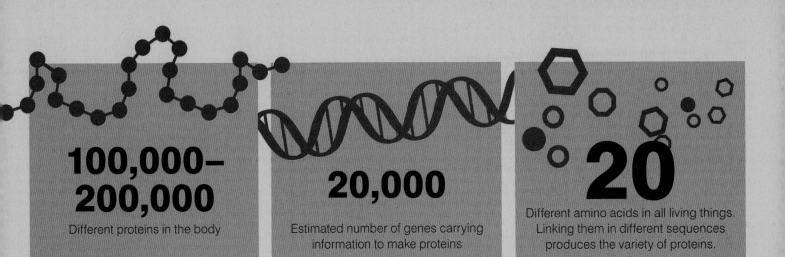

100,000–200,000

Different proteins in the body

20,000

Estimated number of genes carrying information to make proteins

20

Different amino acids in all living things. Linking them in different sequences produces the variety of proteins.

SECOND STAGE:
TRANSLATION IN THE CYTOPLASM

mRNA's coded information is used for protein synthesis, assisted by a ribosome and tRNAs (transfer RNAs)

7 Ribosome joins amino acid to assembled chain

6 tRNA brings correct amino acid specified by the codon

8 Chain of amino acids lengthens to form a protein

Free amino acids

HOW GENES SPECIALIZE

Each cell has a full and complete set of genes, so how do different cells take on their varied appearances and functions? Answer: Not all the genes are active or switched on. Usually, essential "housekeeping" genes are working for basic functions like building organelles and dealing with energy and wastes. But most other genes are switched off or suppressed—apart from those for the cell's specific function. For instance, a red blood cell has its housekeeping genes working, and also those to make oxygen-carrying hemoglobin, while most of the rest are suppressed.

STAGE 1: THE GENETIC INFORMATION

Chromosome 11
Hemoglobin subunit beta gene, HBB.
Location 11p15.5 (chromosome 11, short or p arm, position 15.5).

Chromosome 16
Hemoglobin subunit alpha 1 gene, HBA1.
Hemoglobin subunit alpha 2 gene, HBA2.
Location 16p13.3 (chromosome 16, short or p arm, position 13.3).

p p Location 11p15.5

p p Location 16p13.3

Production of beta globin chain

STAGE 2: MAKING THE PROTEIN SUBUNITS

mRNA assembled using HBB as template

mRNA is "read" by ribosome, which assembles amino acid building-blocks.

Chromosome 11

DNA unzipped to expose HBB gene

STAGE 3: ASSEMBLING THE HEMOGLOBIN MOLECULE

Primary structure
Sequence of 146 amino acids for one beta globin chain.

140 141 142 143 144 145 146

Secondary structure
Sequence takes on bends and kinks due to angles of bonds between amino acids, forming an alpha helix.

3 7 11
2 4 6 8 10 12 14
1 5 9 13

Tertiary structure
Long chain of amino acids (polypeptide) takes on folds, loops, and sheets to give full three-dimensional shape of beta globin.

Quaternary structure
Alpha, beta, and other subunits are assembled to produce complete, fully working hemoglobin protein.

Iron atom in hem group

HEMOGLOBIN WITHIN A RED BLOOD CELL:

280,000,000
Hemoglobin molecules per red blood cell

Hemoglobin molecules in cytoplasm of red blood cell

1/3
of the volume of a red blood cell is hemoglobin

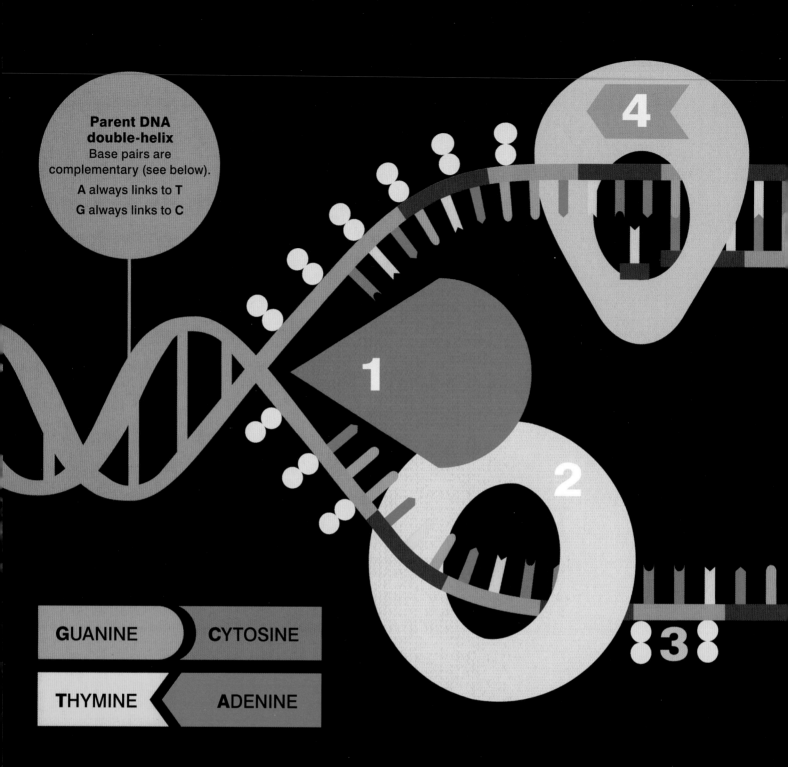

Parent DNA double-helix
Base pairs are complementary (see below).

A always links to **T**
G always links to **C**

GUANINE   CYTOSINE

THYMINE   ADENINE

DNA DOUBLE-UP

No cells live for ever. They divide to produce offspring cells, as shown on the next page. The key to this is copying or replicating the genes, which are chromosomes consisting of lengths of DNA, deoxyribonucleic acid. This allows each offspring cell to receive its full set of genes and continue its parent's work. DNA replication underlies almost every process and event in the body, starting from the amazing development of the body from its first set of DNA in its first single cell, the fertilized egg, through to everyday cell division to replace skin, blood, and other worn-out cells.

1: Helicase
Enzyme to unwind and separate or "unzip" the two existing or parent DNA strands at the links between the bases.

2: Primase and RNA primer
Primase enzyme makes RNA primer, the start point for making the new complementary partner or offspring DNA strand.

3: Binding proteins
Protect the exposed bases to stop them relinking, detaching, or degenerating.

4: DNA polymerase
Enzyme that "reads" existing bases and "clips" new bases, sugars, and phosphates together to form new complementary strand.

5: Leading strand
The existing DNA strand along which DNA polymerase moves continuously to form the lengthening new strand.

6: Lagging strand
DNA polymerase only works in one direction along the DNA backbone, so goes "backward" in a steplike manner on this strand.

7: Okazaki fragments
Short sections of DNA newly made on the existing DNA lagging strand which will be joined by DNA ligase.

8: DNA polymerase and DNA ligase
"Backstitch" Okazaki fragments together to form one long new complementary partner on the existing lagging strand.

9: Offspring DNA
Two identical double-helix lengths, each with one parent DNA strand and one new complementary DNA partner strand.

HOW CELLS DIVIDE

Cells do not arise spontaneously from nonliving matter. (Except, as biologists theorize, more than three billion years ago when they first evolved.) Instead, each cell comes from a pre-existing cell by the process of cell division—sometimes known, confusingly, as cell multiplication. This nearly always produces two cells from one, as the original or parent cell gives rise to two offspring or sibling cells. The key to such division is splitting of the nucleus, known as mitosis. Prior to this, all of the genetic material, DNA, is duplicated, so that each offspring cell receives a full set. (Division to make the sex cells, eggs and sperm, is slightly different—see page 180.)

INTERPHASE
DNA of chromosomes spread out and winding, genes active. Also DNA duplicates.

PROPHASE
DNA of each chromosome coils and "condenses" to become visible. Nuclear membrane disintegrates. Spindle forms from centrosomes and microtubules.

METAPHASE
Microtubules attach to chromosomes. Chromosomes align at center or equator of cell.

ANAPHASE
Pairs of duplicated chromosomes separate, pulled by microtubules to opposite ends of the cell.

TELOPHASE
Chromosomes reach their positions in each sibling cell. Nuclear membrane reforms in each sibling cell.

80

10

4

1

3–7

CELL DIVISION

Figures shown average % of
a cell's life spent in each stage.

CYTOKINESIS

Division of the whole
parent cell into two sibling
cells. Timing varies but
may start early in mitosis.
Contractile ring around the
middle pinches the cell,
forming a cleavage furrow.
Two sibling cells finally
become independent units.

THE LIVES OF CELLS

Each of the body's 200-plus types of cells has its own programed time for existence, before being replaced with more of its kind from that tissue's rapidly multiplying stem cells. In general, hard physical wear or chemical exposure means faster turnover. Deep in the brain are the longest survivors—the neurons that give us thoughts, feelings, and memories. As a rough guide to their prodigious numbers, the cells turned over in one second in the body, laid end to end, would stretch more than half a mile.

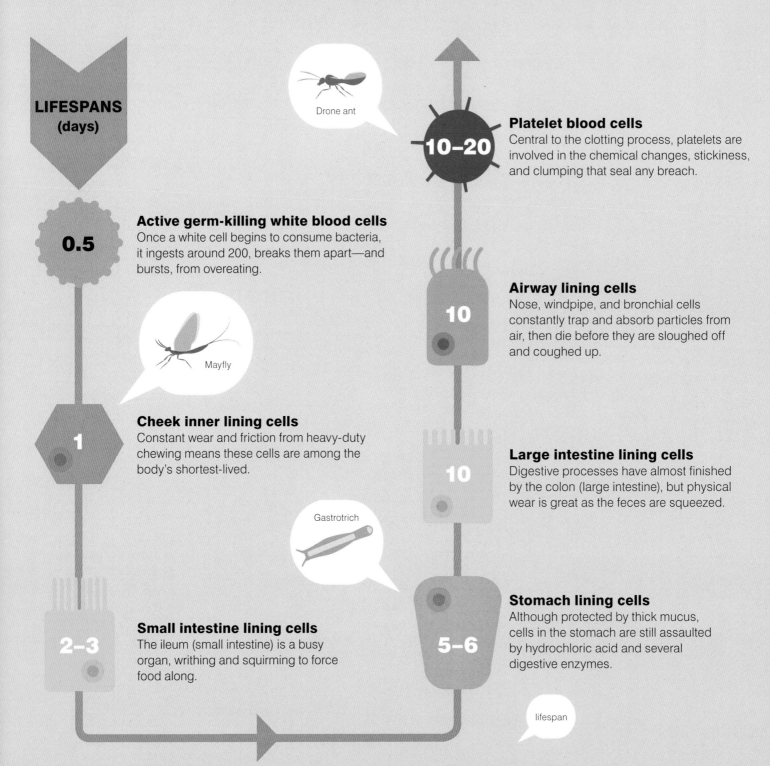

LIFESPANS (days)

Drone ant

10–20

Platelet blood cells
Central to the clotting process, platelets are involved in the chemical changes, stickiness, and clumping that seal any breach.

0.5

Active germ-killing white blood cells
Once a white cell begins to consume bacteria, it ingests around 200, breaks them apart—and bursts, from overeating.

Mayfly

10

Airway lining cells
Nose, windpipe, and bronchial cells constantly trap and absorb particles from air, then die before they are sloughed off and coughed up.

1

Cheek inner lining cells
Constant wear and friction from heavy-duty chewing means these cells are among the body's shortest-lived.

10

Large intestine lining cells
Digestive processes have almost finished by the colon (large intestine), but physical wear is great as the feces are squeezed.

Gastrotrich

2–3

Small intestine lining cells
The ileum (small intestine) is a busy organ, writhing and squirming to force food along.

5–6

Stomach lining cells
Although protected by thick mucus, cells in the stomach are still assaulted by hydrochloric acid and several digestive enzymes.

lifespan

Retinal cells, eye
10–20

Average lives of the light-sensing or photoreceptor cells, rods, and cones, mean a constant slow turnover in the delicate eye lining.

Epidermal (outer skin) cells
20–30

Physical wear, friction, and minor injuries mean the whole outer layer of skin, the epidermis, replaces itself at least monthly.

Red blood cells
120

Bone marrow produces more than two million every second, as the same number's minerals are recycled, especially by the spleen and liver.

Liver cells
150

Known as hepatocytes, liver cells are multitaskers, handling all kinds of minerals and nutrients, as well as storing vitamins.

Pancreatic cells
350 (1 year)

Some pancreatic cells make the hormones insulin and glycogen, others produce digestive enzymes for the small intestine.

Mouse

30,000
(80 years)

Brain neurons
Their enormously complex architecture, with thousands of synapses (connections), mean cerebral neurons can last almost a lifetime.

22,000
(60 years)

Memory white cells
After an infection, a few memory T and B cells circulate for years, even decades, ready to spring into action and fight the same disease again.

African elephant

Horse

10,000
(25 years)

Bone maintenance cells
Osteocytes have complex shapes, like a three-dimensional spider with over 100 legs. They keep bone minerals topped up and turning over.

5,500 (15 years)

Skeletal muscle cells
Muscle cells or myocytes are big multicells made of many smaller cells fused into one unit, with diameters up to one millimeter.

500
(16 months)

Lung lining cells
The tiny air sacs, alveoli, accumulate bits of dust and other debris at a slow rate, and so are replaced every year or two.

HOW GENES INTERACT

The human genome has 46 chromosomes, or lengths of DNA, as 23 pairs. That is, there are two chromosome 1s, two 2s, and so on. Does this mean two identical copies of each gene, one on each chromosome of the pair? Like most of genetics, the answers are yes, no, and maybe. In some people, the two versions, or alleles, of a particular gene are identical. In others, the two alleles are different. One is stronger or dominant, and it overpowers its weaker or recessive counterpart. An example is the gene for the blood group Rhesus, RH. It has alleles for being Rhesus positive, RH+, or Rhesus negative, RH−. Oh, and much much more (see right).

Location: 1p36.11

(chromosome 1, short or p arm, position 36.11)

Blood group Rh gene

Gene name: RHD (and others)
Length: 58,000 base pairs

Product

Name: Rhesus D protein RHD on red blood cells
Length: 416 amino acids

+ D+ allele
Makes RHD

RHD present.
Blood RH+

− D- allele does
not make RHD

RHD absent.
Blood RH-

The three possibilities
The three possible combinations of RHD genes depend on the alleles on the two chromosome 1s. One of these comes from the mother and the other from the father. D+ is stronger or more dominant, D− is weaker or recessive.

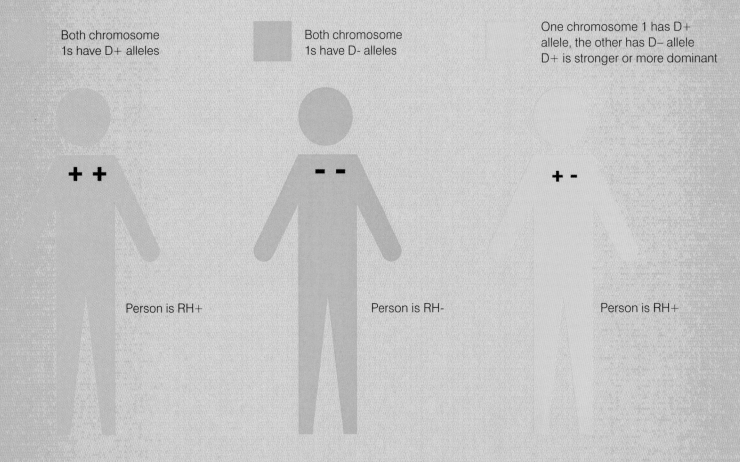

Both chromosome
1s have D+ alleles

Both chromosome
1s have D- alleles

One chromosome 1 has D+
allele, the other has D− allele
D+ is stronger or more dominant

+ +

− −

+ -

Person is RH+

Person is RH-

Person is RH+

GENETICS IS NEVER THAT SIMPLE

The explanation here of the **Rhesus blood group** is very simplified.

There are not just two alleles for the RHD gene, but more than 50.

This means there are many RHD proteins, like Weak D, Partial D, DEL, and several more.

And not all Weak Ds are the same. There's Weak D type 1, Weak D type 2, Weak D type 4, Weak D type 11, Weak D type 57, and more.

On top of all this, RHD is only one of several genes in the rhesus family.

Others are RHCE, RHAG, RHBG, and RHCG, some on different chromosomes.

These make a variety of other proteins such as C, E, c, and e.

And remember that Rhesus is only one blood group. There are also ABO on chromosome 9, MNS on chromosome 4, L (Lewis), K (Kell)— more than 30 groups in all.

That's just one tiny glimpse of why genetics is so complicated.

INHERITING GENES

Genes are inherited directly from our parents. As mentioned, each cell in the body has two full sets of genes, as pairs of chromosomes 1 to 23. These are replicates of replicates of replicates many times over, via cell division, from the original first two sets of chromosomes. One of these original sets was in the mother's egg cell and the other in the father's sperm cell (see page 182). See how different combinations of different versions, or alleles, of a gene produce different results—but smile first!

DIMPLES

These small cheek pits or indentations are probably caused by a dominant version or allele of the dimples gene, let's call it **+**. Not having dimples is the recessive allele, **−**. Remember that only one of the mother's two dimples genes can go into each egg, likewise, one from the father into each sperm. How they combine is all down to chance.

SCENARIO 1

DIMPLES

NO DIMPLES

SCENARIO 2

SCENARIO 3

THE GENETIC EVE

In a cell, each "powerpack" mitochondrion has short lengths of DNA, called mDNA or mtDNA. When a sperm joins an egg at fertilization, it does not contribute mitochondria. So all of a body's mtDNA came solely from the mother. Studies of mtDNA changes or mutations trace our human species, *Homo sapiens*, back to a theoretical female Genetic Eve (Mitochondrial Eve) in Africa 200,000 years ago.

Original mtDNA

Slight change or mutation in mtDNA

Another slight change or mutation in mtDNA

SENSITIVE BODY

Newborn

17

2.5

3-year-old

22

5.5

EYES HAVE IT

For sighted people, up to two-thirds of sensory information about the outside world enters through the eyes. Each of these real-time-roving, super-sharp-seeing, full-color-capable living cameras is an intricate marvel of structures and tissues packed into a jelly-filled ball just 24 mm (1 inch) across. Light rays are bent, or refracted, through a series of almost perfectly transparent substances before they are detected by the retina, which then fires off nerve signals to the brain. To achieve such minimal light obstruction, the transparent tissues—cornea, lens, and aqueous and vitreous humors (liquids)—have the distinction of being the most blood-free in the body. By simple diffusion or seepage, the cornea gains nutrients from tear fluid and oxygen from air; the lens gets them from fluids around it.

Eyeball size

The eye is the organ nearest its final adult size at birth. Because of the way spheres enlarge, from newborn to adult its diameter increases by 41%, yet its volume enlarges by 188%.

Adult (15+)

24

7.2

Diameter in mm   Volume in ml

VITREOUS

IRIS

Thickness ▼ (mm)

0.25 — **CONJUNCTIVA**
Sensitive covering of eye, washed regularly by tear fluid and blinking

0.35 — **RETINA**
Inner light-sensitive lining

0.5 — **CORNEA**
Clear, domed front of eye

Seconds to travel from an object 100 feet away

← **000,000,1** —
(one-tenth of one-millionth of a second)

1–1.5 — **AQUEOUS**
Fluid between the cornea and lens, on either side of the iris

4 — **LENS**
Elastic, adjusts to fine-focus light rays

2 4 8 **PUPIL**
Hole in center of iris (Diameter)

The dimmer the light the wider the pupil

INSIDE THE RETINA

Our multicolor, in-depth, continuously moving image of the world is sensed by an area not much larger than a thumbnail. The retina is packed with light-sensitive rod and cone cells, nerve fibers leading from them, a layer of nerve cells to network information from these fibers, another three layers of nerve cells for further information processing, and a branching web of blood vessels to supply all of these with oxygen and nourishment. A noticeable hurdle is that the cones and rods are almost at the base of the retina. So light must pass through all the other structures to get to them, causing plentiful obstructions and shadows. This could be viewed as a design fault, but the processing nerve cell layers and the brain itself rapidly become adept at computing what's likely to be there, to fill gaps.

EYE VERSUS TV SCREEN

- Standard definition
- High definition (HD)
- Ultra-high definition (UHD-4K)

1 million image units

Nerve fibers

Ganglion cells

Bipolar cells

Horizontal cells

Rods

Cones

FIND YOUR BLIND SPOT!

Everybody has a blind spot, a point on the back of the retina where about one million ganglion cell nerve fibers gather to leave the retina as the optic nerve. There are no rods or cones here, so it corresponds to the "blind spot."

Close your right eye and look at the cross with your left eye. As you look at the cross, move the page forward and backward until the eye blinks it out of existence.

Try the same with this diagram. What happens to the black line when the cross disappears?

What happens when the eye is surrounded by color?

What happens when the eye is surrounded by dots?

EYE TO BRAIN

What the eye sees is only part of what the mind's eye sees. We live in the past because of a gap, some 50–100 milliseconds (0.05–0.1 seconds), between rods and cones in the retina responding to light rays, and the mind's conscious perception of the image their nerve signals represent. Part of this delay are signals traveling through the networking cells of the retina, along the optic nerve, through the brain's optic chiasm (crossover) and nerve pathways to the main visual centers at the lower rear, then being shared around to different accessory centers, each of which examines its own aspect of the scene. From all this information, the mind constructs its own version of visual reality, looking backward and forward in time, analyzing and surmising, coordinating and correlating, always on the go but always lagging slightly behind.

FIELDS OF VISION

Side-to-side (lateral)

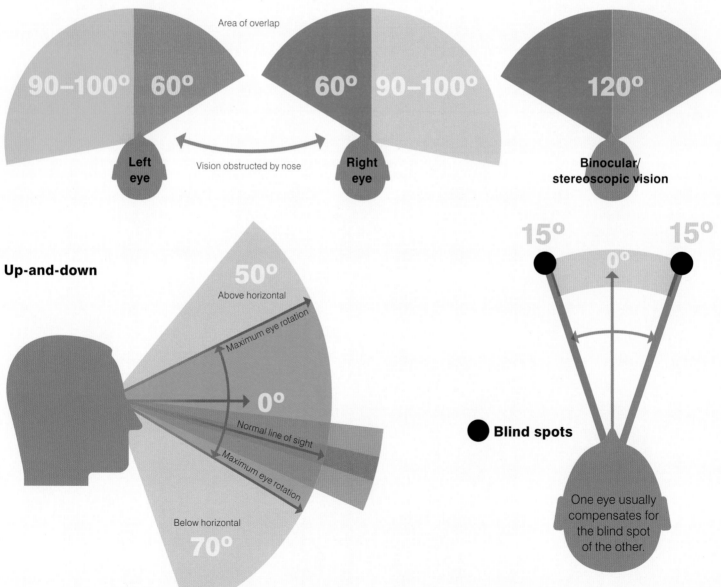

Area of overlap

90–100°   60°   60°   90–100°   120°

Left eye   Vision obstructed by nose   Right eye   Binocular/ stereoscopic vision

Up-and-down

15°   15°

0°

50°
Above horizontal

Maximum eye rotation

0°
Normal line of sight

Maximum eye rotation

Below horizontal
70°

● **Blind spots**

One eye usually compensates for the blind spot of the other.

THE OPTIC NERVE

More than 1,000,000 nerve fibers, more than any other sensory nerve!

When the eye detects an electronic flash lasting one millisecond (0.001 seconds), the brain reports that it persists from anywhere between 100 and 400 milliseconds (0.1 and 0.4 seconds).

2 inches

Optic Chiasm

Lateral geniculate nucleus (in thalamus), major relay station for visual nerve signals

Left visual centers receive right half of field of view from each eye

Right visual centers receive left half of field of view from each eye

SOUND SENSE

A world awash with sound and noise comes from a little snail-shaped body part just ⅖ inch tall. It is deep in the inner ear but could comfortably perch on a little fingernail. The cochlea receives vibrations from the air via the eardrum and ear ossicle bones, and converts them into electrical nerve signals. Its key components are a row of about 3,500 inner hair cells arranged along a flexible sheet, the basilar membrane, winding inside the cochlea. As vibrations shake the sheet, the microhairs on the tops of these cells—which are embedded in a jellylike "roof" above—are bent and twisted. These ultrafine motions cause the hair cells to generate nerve signals that zoom along the auditory nerve to the brain's hearing centers.

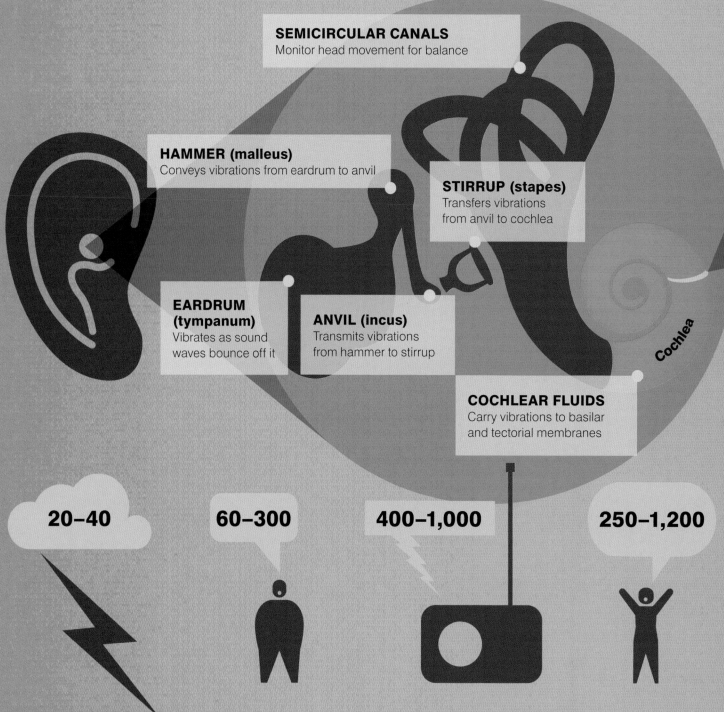

SEMICIRCULAR CANALS
Monitor head movement for balance

HAMMER (malleus)
Conveys vibrations from eardrum to anvil

STIRRUP (stapes)
Transfers vibrations from anvil to cochlea

EARDRUM (tympanum)
Vibrates as sound waves bounce off it

ANVIL (incus)
Transmits vibrations from hammer to stirrup

COCHLEAR FLUIDS
Carry vibrations to basilar and tectorial membranes

Cochlea

20–40

60–300

400–1,000

250–1,200

CROSS-SECTION OF THE COCHLEA

Scala vestibuli

Scala media

Scala timpani

Vibrations of membranes stimulate hair cells

0.05 mm

12,000 OUTER HAIR CELLS
Receive nerve signals and move their microhairs to tense the basilar/tectorial membranes, increasing sensitivity of inner hair cells

0.03 mm

3,500 INNER HAIR CELLS
Vibrations cause microhairs to bend, producing nerve signals

HIGHS AND LOWS
Sound frequency or pitch is measured in vibrations per second, Hz (Hertz).

300–600

27.5

1,000–8,000

6,000

4,186

LIFE IN STEREO

After sight, sound is the body's most informative sense; and with smell, it's one of three senses that works at a distance.

THE SPEED OF SOUND

SECONDS

▶ 1 2 3 4 5

MILE

1,000 YARDS

370 YARDS

Sound speed is one million times slower than light speed, so ears use a delay system to gauge direction and distance. It's based on the gap between the ears, which means sounds from one side, such as music, reach the nearer ear less than 0.001 seconds before the far ear. These sounds are also quieter and more muffled in the far ear. Yet the brain's hearing centers detect all this in a split second. The brain then directs the neck muscles to turn the head to that side, to… face the music.

Sound waves are varying regions of high and low air pressure.

5½ inches

0.001 second delay

LOUD AND LOUDER

The sound intensity scale in decibels (dB) is not an equal stepwise progression scale, but a logarithmic one to base 10. It means 20 dB is 10 times more intense or powerful than 10 dB (not twice), 30 dB is 100 times (not three), and so on.

170
Hearing loss inevitable

140
Jet engine at 100 feet

120
Ear pain likely

110
Loud music concert, nearby thunder

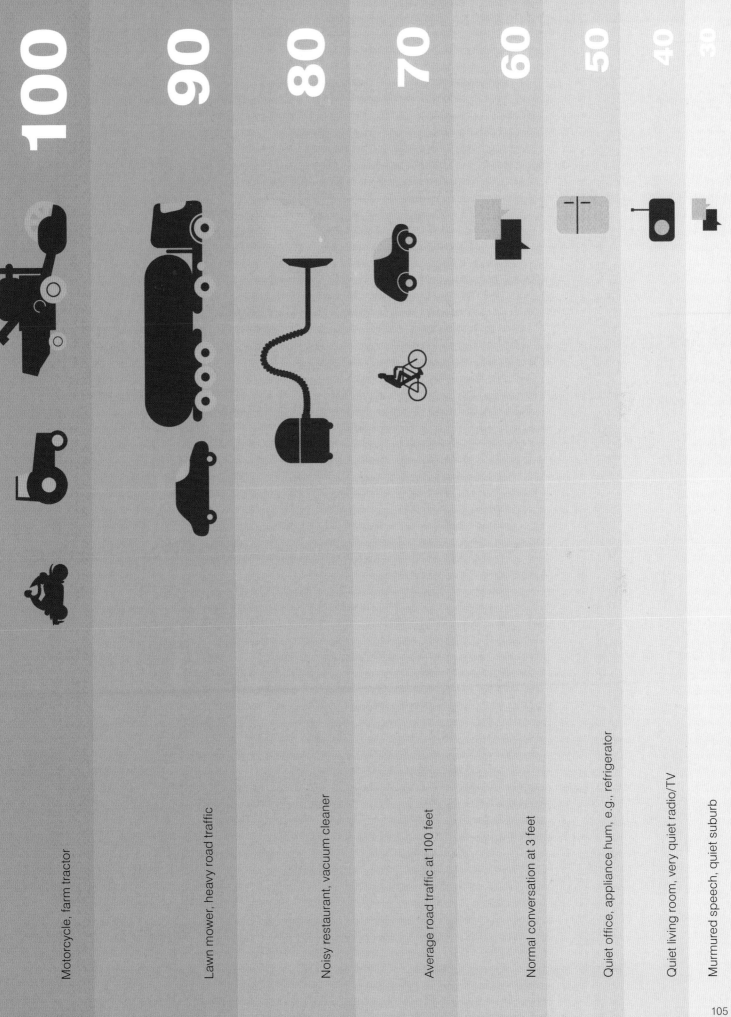

100 Motorcycle, farm tractor

90 Lawn mower, heavy road traffic

80 Noisy restaurant, vacuum cleaner

70 Average road traffic at 100 feet

60 Normal conversation at 3 feet

50 Quiet office, appliance hum, e.g., refrigerator

40 Quiet living room, very quiet radio/TV

30 Murmured speech, quiet suburb

SCENTS SENSE

Smell, or olfaction, is the third-most informative noncontact sense. It brings information about possibly dangerous vapors and gases in the air, as well as scents and aromas concerned with foods, drinks, plants, animals, and others of our kind—good and bad. Smells can give intense pleasure but also cause strong reactions, such as retching. More than other senses, olfaction is hardwired to parts of the brain concerned with memories and emotions, which is why scents and aromas provoke such powerful feelings.

THE FOOD EXPERIENCE

Taste and smell are separate sensory systems but closely mingled in conscious perception to create the overall "food experience" of each mouthful.

Estimated contribution to total food experience (%):

15 Memories

15 Taste

10 Immediate circumstances

60 Smell

OLFACTORY EPITHELIUM

This area in the roof of the nasal chamber is 1 sq inch per side of nose and contains 5–10 million olfactory cells (olfactory receptor neurons). It produces fluid to dissolve odorant molecules and enable detection.

NASAL CHAMBER

Divided into two halves, left and right, by nasal septal cartilage. The lining warms, humidifies, and filters particles from incoming air. Turbinates (conchae) are bony ridges directing airflow to olfactory epithelium.

ODORANTS

Invisible odor or smell particles (mostly molecules) float on air currents. They carry information in their size, shape, and electrical charges, moving via the orthonasal route through nostrils from general surroundings and the retronasal route around the rear of the palate from food/drink in mouth.

5 NERVE FIBERS OF OLFACTORY CELLS

The nerve fibers collect into bundles of 20–30. They pass through cribriform plate, a perforated region of the ethmoid bone of the skull. They convey nerve signals to the olfactory bulb. They are regarded (sometimes with olfactory bulb and tract) as the olfactory nerve, also called cranial nerve I (1).

$^2/_5$ in

6

5

4

6 OLFACTORY BULB

This lobelike extension of forebrain consists of five main cell layers. It decodes, filters, coordinates, enhances, and processes nerve information from olfactory cells.

OLFACTORY RECEPTORS

These are molecules embedded in exposed surfaces of olfactory cells, and they are stimulated on contact with a suitable odorant molecule—"lock and key" mechanism. Olfactory receptor cells generate nerve signals, which are sent along the nerve fibers to the olfactory bulb.

7

OLFACTORY TRACT

This is the nerve fibers linking the olfactory bulb and brain.

PRIMARY OLFACTORY CORTEX

Main region dealing with smell information situated on the inner temporal lobe of the brain. It has close links with the regions involving emotions and memories.

8

$1–1^1/_5$ in

Volume (cc)
15–20

BEST POSSIBLE TASTE

In everyday experience, taste or gustation is inextricably mixed with smell, especially when savoring a fabulous meal. However, it is a separate sensory system—and is not all it seems. Nerve signals from its chief sensors, taste buds, provide only part of taste information. Nontaste features such as heat/cold and physical texture—rough, slippery, squashy—add massively to the overall sensory impressions gained from foods. Researchers are finding that identifying tastes is similar in complexity to pinpointing smells. Many gustatory receptors fire many nerve signals at many rates when stimulated by many tastant substances (ones that stimulate the taste buds). The brain uses much decoding and pattern recognition to sort out the results. *Bon appetit*!

10,000
taste buds in total on the tongue, mouth lining, inner lips, gums, and upper throat

Vallate
200–300
X 8–15

1

TONGUE
This is the body's most flexible muscle complex. Its upper surface bears papillae of various shapes.

Foliate
110–120
X 10–15

4,000–6,000
taste buds on the tongue

2

PAPILLAE
These help to grip and move food for chewing. There are four main kinds:
Vallate: large and circular;
Foliate: foldlike or flaplike;
Fungiform: mostly at the front, also main surface and sides, reddish in color;
Filiform: threadlike or tufted, and covering much of surface.

Filiform
0
X more than 50

X Number of papillae on the tongue

⬤ Number of taste buds in each papilla

Fungiform
1–20
X 200

Foliate papillae

← **0.03–0.04 mm**

GUSTATORY (TASTE RECEPTOR) CELLS

4

Tastants enter through taste pore. Threadlike taste hairs (microvilli) at the top detect tastants using receptors, in a similar way to odorants.

Taste pore **0.003–0.006 mm**

supporting cell

supporting cell

50–100
per taste bud

NERVE FIBERS OF OLFACTORY CELLS

5

These carry nerve signals from gustatory cells. They gather at each bud and then into larger bundles within the tongue.

GUSTATORY NERVE PATHWAYS

 6

There is no single taste nerve. The facial nerve, also called cranial nerve VII (7), carries signals from the front two-thirds of the tongue, while the glossopharyngeal, or cranial nerve IX (9), serves the rear third. Other areas of the mouth are supplied by the vagus or cranial nerve X (10).

PRIMARY GUSTATORY CORTEX

 7

This is found on the inner insular and frontal lobes of the brain and is the main region dealing with taste information. It identifies tastes using pattern recognition, as for smell. It has close links with regions involving hunger, appetite, and sweating.

The cortex is the main folded surface of the brain, where nerve cells interconnect.

SKIN AND SURFACE SENSORS

These are specialized nerve endings, regarded as single cells, each giving off a nerve fiber.

20–100
Krause
Temperature changes,
especially cold

5–20
Merkel
Light touch, light pressure,
angular features such as edges

100–300
Meissner
Light touch, slow vibrations,
surface textures

Wilhelm Krause (German 1833–1910)

Friedrich Merkel (German 1845–1919)

Georg Meissner (German 1829–1905)

TOUCHY FEELY

The skin's visible surface is actually dead cells designed for wear and protection, but just beneath teem millions of sensory cells. "Touch" is far too simple a term. Types of contact distinguish rough or smooth, wet or dry, rigid or yielding, warm or cool, and many other features. These derive from floods of nerve signals from six main kinds of sensory cells. The signals pass through the bodywide nerve network to a strip on the brain's surface, the touch center (officially the somatosensory cortex), where they register in conscious perception.

Sizes in μm (micrometers) 1 μm = 0.001 mm

100–500
Ruffini
Slow-acting and sustained pressure,
temperature changes, especially heat

Angelo Ruffini (Italian 1864–1929)

500–1,200
Pacini
Fast vibrations,
strong pressure

Filippo Pacini (Italian 1812–1883)

Free nerve endings
Various forms of touch,
temperature changes, pain

Why the names?
Several skin sensors were named after the
19th-century anatomists, biologists, or similar
scientists who identified and studied them
under the microscope.

INNER SENSE

Without looking, what are your arms and legs doing? Are they crossed, folded, straight, bent, stationary, moving? Knowing or being aware of the positions, postures, and movements of body parts is termed proprioception. It is a sense we rarely consider, but its second-by-second reports are vital in daily life. Its inputs are various tiny sensory organs and nerve endings that are mechanoreceptors (responding to physical forces). They are located almost everywhere within organs and tissues, especially in muscles and their tendons, and inside joint ligaments and capsules. Some are similar to those in the skin, such as Ruffini and Pacinci sensors (see page 111). As with the skin's touch messages, these proprioceptors send signals along nerves to the brain, where they are integrated with other sensory information to give an awareness of position and motion for each and every body part.

MUSCLE SPINDLES

Dozens to hundreds in main body or belly of a muscle. Respond to changes in length, detecting squeezing (compression), and stretching (tension)

CAPSULE PROPRIOCEPTORS

In joint capsules, the fibrous casings around the bone ends in a joint. Similar to Ruffini and Pacini sensors in skin

0.5–1 mm

NEUROTENDON (GOLGI) SPINDLES

In tendons that connect muscles to bones. Respond to changes in squeezing (compression) as muscle contracts

0.1–1 mm

0.1–1 mm

LIGAMENT PROPRIOCEPTORS

In stretchy ligaments that link bones in a joint. Similar to Ruffini and Pacini sensors in skin

PROPRIOCEPTIVE TESTS

Try these tests to demonstrate the importance of your inner sense, but note:

- First do the test quite quickly, without too much preparation or thinking.
- Then do it more slowly, concentrating on the positions of your arms and hands.
- With each further attempt, see how you can make your attention focus more precisely on proprioception.

1 Hold arms and hands straight to front

2 Close eyes

3 With left hand, touch tip of nose with thumb and each finger in turn

4 Do same for right hand

You will need:

1 Sit at a table, and hold down a piece of paper with one hand.

2 Close eyes and keep them closed for duration of exercise.

3 With a pencil in your other hand, mark an X on the paper.

4 Swap the paper-holding and pencil-holding hands.

5 Mark a second X as near as possible to first X.

6 Open your eyes.

BALANCING ACT

Balance is sometimes characterized as a mysterious sixth sense. In one respect, balance does engage the senses—in fact, almost all of the main sensory arrangements, plus others based deep in the ear. These inner-ear structures go by the general name of the vestibular system. It is based on the vestibule chamber of the inner ear with its offshoots of three semicircular canals, utricle, and saccule. Their minutest detections, in parts known as the macula and ampulla, run along similar lines to hearing's cochlea, as hair cells fire off nerve signals when their microhairs are physically triggered. But balance is a much wider and continuously ongoing issue. It correlates constant inputs from eyes, skin, and proprioceptive sensors, with continual outputs controlling muscles ranging from eye-movers to leg-stabilizers.

INNER EARS

Head movements cause fluid inside the ear to bend hair cells in cupulae of canals and maculae of vestibule chambers

Semicircular canals, utricle, and saccule:

cupulae
of canals

macula
of utricle

macula
of saccule

EYES

Register horizontals and verticals

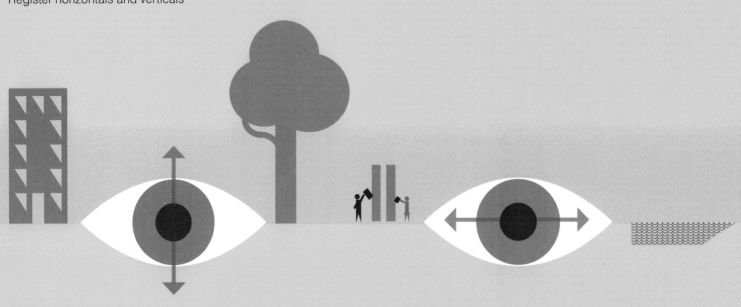

PROPRIOCEPTORS
Pressure and tension sensors are found in:

Joint ligaments

Tendons

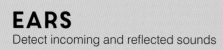

Muscles

SKIN
Senses pressure, for example, pushing with hands and arms or the tilt on the soles of the feet

EARS
Detect incoming and reflected sounds

Sounds alter with
position of head relative
to nearby surfaces

MAKING SENSE

Each main sense sends its nerve signals to its own region of the brain's thin outer layer, the cortex. But on the way, these nerve signals and the information they represent go through many stages of processing, decoding, analyzing, and being shared around. And once at the cortex, the information is likewise distributed and coordinated with other sensory centers for memories, recognition, naming, associations, emotions, decisions, and reactions. Which is why an aroma familiar from childhood conjures up sights, sounds, tastes, feelings, even a whole recreation of a scene from long ago. Pine woodland, seaside spray, theme park snack, regurgitated baby milk…

Lobes of the brain
The lobes of the main brain parts, the cerebral hemispheres, are anatomical areas known since antiquity. They are demarcated by deep grooves called fissures or sulci.

FRONTAL
- conscious thought • self-awareness
- decisions • personality • memories
- aspects of smell and speech
- planning and controlling movements

CENTRAL SULCUS
Separates frontal and parietal lobes

PARIETAL
- coordinating sensory information
- visual-spatial aspects • various aspects of touch
- taste • aspects of speech • proprioception

LATERAL SULCUS (FISSURE)
Separates frontal and parietal lobes from temporal lobe

LIMBIC
- emotions
- memories
- experiences

PARIETO-OCCIPITAL SULCUS
Separates parietal and occipital lobes

OCCIPITAL
- sight and associated, features
- sensory coordination • memories

TEMPORAL
- hearing • aspects of smell and sight
- coordination of sensory information • speech
- language • short- and long-term memories

Sensitive brain

The main areas for receiving sensory information are each demarcated on a particular lobe. Oddly, the surface of the brain itself has no touch sensory cells and so, if poked or prodded, feels no contact (although consciousness may be affected).

TOUCH MAP

The somatosensory cortex (touch centers) on each side of the brain form a striplike body map. More sensitive parts such as lips and fingertips occupy more area on the cortex.

HIP

TRUNK

HEAD & NECK

SHOULDER

LEG

UPPER ARM

ELBOW

FOREARM

WRIST

HAND

FOOT

TOES

GENITALS

FINGERS

5
4
3
2
1

EYE

NOSE

FACE

UPPER LIP

BOTH LIPS

LOWER LIP

TEETH & GUMS

TONGUE

THROAT

Many nerve fibers cross over in the lower brain. So, touch nerve signals from the right side of the body go to the brain's left cortex, and vice versa.

COORDINATED BODY

FEELING NERVOUS

The body's billions of cells, hundreds of tissues and dozens of organs work together as a harmonious whole – but how? There are two chief bodywide coordination-control-command systems: nervous, and hormonal or endocrine. The first works mainly by tiny electrical signals whizzing along wire-like nerves, while the second is based on chemical substances called hormones. The brain is the hub of both systems.

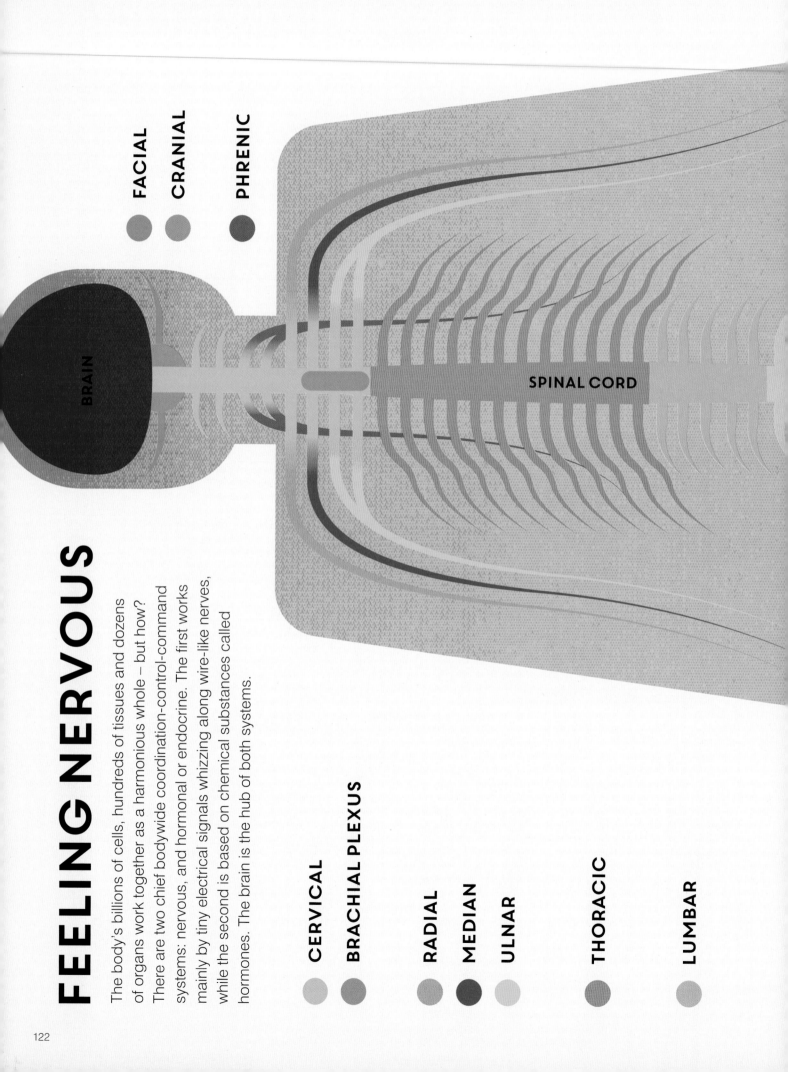

FACIAL

CRANIAL

PHRENIC

BRAIN

SPINAL CORD

CERVICAL

BRACHIAL PLEXUS

RADIAL

MEDIAN

ULNAR

THORACIC

LUMBAR

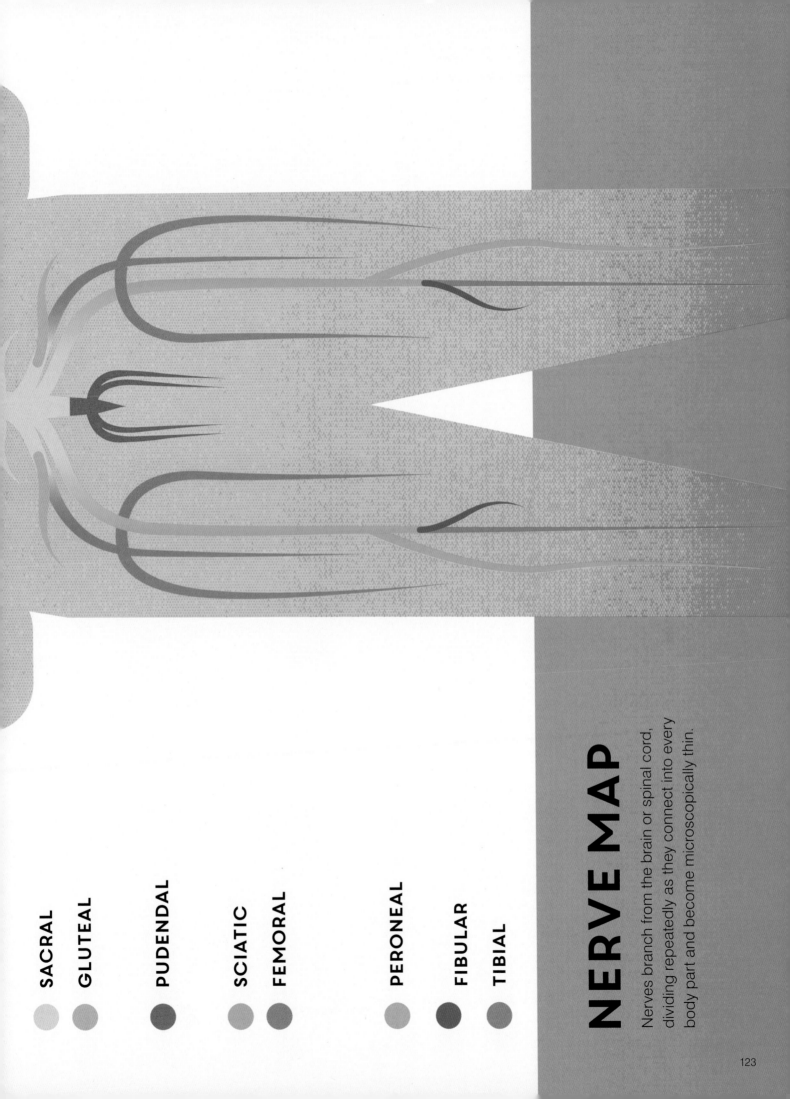

NERVE MAP

Nerves branch from the brain or spinal cord, dividing repeatedly as they connect into every body part and become microscopically thin.

- SACRAL
- GLUTEAL
- PUDENDAL
- SCIATIC
- FEMORAL
- PERONEAL
- FIBULAR
- TIBIAL

2   3   4

1

5

HEADFUL OF NERVES

Forty-three pairs of nerves (left and right) branch from the brain and spinal cord out into the body. Twelve of these come directly from the brain and are known as cranial nerves; the other 31 pairs from the cord are spinal nerves. Cranial nerves carry information from the main senses to the brain, and signals from the brain to the muscles of the face, head, and neck—and, in one case, the heart, lungs, and stomach.

motor: signals from brain to muscles ▽

sensory: signals from senses to brain △

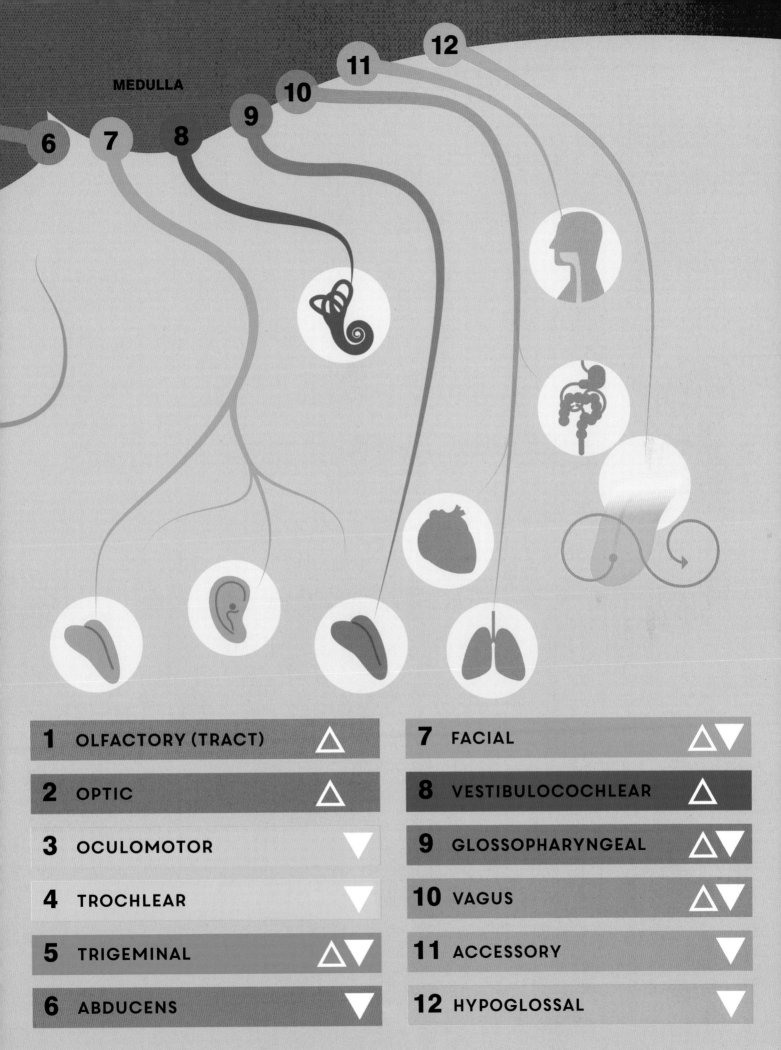

MEDULLA

1 OLFACTORY (TRACT)	△		7 FACIAL	△▼
2 OPTIC	△		8 VESTIBULOCOCHLEAR	△
3 OCULOMOTOR	▼		9 GLOSSOPHARYNGEAL	△▼
4 TROCHLEAR	▼		10 VAGUS	△▼
5 TRIGEMINAL	△▼		11 ACCESSORY	▼
6 ABDUCENS	▼		12 HYPOGLOSSAL	▼

MIND THE GAP

Nerves all around the body use the same basic communication system. This is chiefly electrical with some chemical stages along the way. A single nerve signal or message is a tiny pulse of electricity that lasts for a tiny amount of time; it is the same for any nerve, at any time, anywhere in the body. The information carried depends on how fast the pulses follow each other, where they come from, and where they go.

1 INCOMING

Nerve signals are gathered by nerve cell's dendrites

Dendrite size range
0.1–5 μm

2 SIGNAL

Also called an action potential, this is caused by electrically charged particles (ions) moving across the cell membrane.

4 OUTGOING

Resulting signals leave cell body along axons (nerve fibers)

Diameter range of axons
0.2–20 μm

0.1VOLTS
1MILLISECOND

3 INTEGRATION

Nerve cell (neuron) receives perhaps millions of signals per second. Some signals reinforce many other interactions, while others cancel them.

Range of nerve cell body size
5–50 μm

Some nerve cells have over

10,000

dendrites totalling several inches in length.

5
IMPROVING CONDUCTION

Myelin sheath coats many axons. The sheath of fatty myelin spirals around the axons. This increases speed as signal "jumps" along the axon. The sheath also prevents the signal from weakening and reduces leakage.

6
AT THE JUNCTION

The junction between nerve cells is called a synapse. The end of each axon does not quite touch the next nerve cell.

Average synaptic gap
0.02 μm

8
ONWARD

The receiver is another nerve cell's dendrite or cell body. Neurotransmitters trigger new electrical signals. Signals travel away from the synapse.

0.1 MILLISECOND
Crossing time

7
CHEMICAL CROSSING

Chemicals called neurotransmitters carry the signal. Each signal can have thousands, even millions, of neurotransmitter molecules.

Longest axons almost
1 yard (toe to spinal cord)

1 μm = micrometer = 0.001 mm = 0.000,001 m (one millionth of a meter)

THE VITAL LINK

The spinal cord is the brain's long, slim, metrolike link into the main body. Thirty-one pairs of spinal nerves branch from it, exiting at joints between the backbones or vertebrae. All the spinal nerves carry sensory information from the skin and inner organs via the spinal cord to the brain, and motor signals from the brain via the spinal cord out to the muscles.

Dermatomes
Each spinal nerve collects touch and other sensory information from a segment-like area of skin and underlying tissue called a dermatome.

CERVICAL
NECK

THORACIC
CHEST
UPPER BACK

LUMBAR
LOWER BACK

SACRAL
HIP

COCCYGEAL
COCCYX
(TAILBONE)

FRONT

BACK

Spinal nerves
These nerves are named after
their adjacent backbones:

1
2
3
4
5
6
7
8

1
2
3
4
5
6
7
8
9
10
11
12

1
2
3
4
5

1
2
3
4
5

1

REFLEXES AND REACTIONS

Often the brain's attention must focus on a particularly important task, like reading this book—or flying a supersonic jet plane. So as not to interrupt, many body parts look after themselves with automatic movements called reflexes. The part responds to a stimulus, such as a touch, by nerve signals that go to the spinal cord and "short-circuit" straight back to muscles to make the necessary movement, leaving the brain to catch up later, if needed. Reactions are quick, purposeful movements that do involve the brain's conscious alertness as it detects a situation, thinks fast, and orders a rapid response.

Stimulus

TYPICAL REACTION TIMES (IN SECONDS)

0.05
Eyeball looks to side and back

0.1
Finger keyboard stroke

0.2
Eye blink

0.3
Fist punch

0.5
Foot kick

Mind's conscious awareness

Brain's subconscious filters

HOW REFLEXES HAPPEN

The body senses a stimulus such as sudden movement, an unfamiliar touch or pain, and orders an action straight away. Nerve signals also go to the brain, where they are filtered subconsciously to see if they are important enough to enter conscious awareness.

– – – – Sensory nerve

– – – – Relay nerve

– – – – Motor nerve

– – – – Relay up spinal cord

POINT TO THE ODD-ONE-OUT

Pointing to the odd-one-out of three objects: **0.7** seconds

Pointing to the odd-one-out of six objects: **1** second

SANS: EMERGENCY!

The sympathetic part of the ANS prepares the body for action, energy use, and self-protection, often called "fright, fight, or flight," along with the hormone system. Most of its control is by the vagus nerve and sympathetic nerve chains (ganglia) alongside the spinal cord.

BLOOD GLUCOSE (SUGAR)
More available for energy

EYE PUPILS
Dilated (widened)

DIGESTIVE ACTIVITY
Reduced

BLOOD PRESSURE
Raised

HEARTBEAT
More rapid

BREATHING
Faster, deeper

MUSCLES
Tensed, ready with extra blood supply

CRANIAL

CERVICAL

THORACAL

LUMBAL

PANS: NORMAL SERVICE

The parasympathetic ANS carries out everyday "housekeeping." Most of its nerve control comes from the brain via the spinal cord. Its actions usually oppose the sympathetic part. In daily life, the two continually balance their effects.

BLOOD GLUCOSE (SUGAR)
Usual amounts available for energy

EYE PUPILS
Constricted (narrowed)

DIGESTIVE ACTIVITY
Appropriate

BLOOD PRESSURE
Standard

HEARTBEAT
Normal

BREATHING
Steady

MUSCLES
Relaxed

SKIN
Pale, due to blood diverted away

URINARY ACTIVITY
Lessened

GANGLIA

SACRAL

SKIN
Usual blood supply

URINARY ACTIVITY
Normal

RUNNING ON AUTO

The human brain is truly astonishing, but even it has limited processing power for information passing through at the level of conscious awareness. Therefore, it offloads much of the body's inner workings, such as digesting food, heartbeat, breathing, and waste collection, to happen automatically under the auspices of the autonomic nervous system or ANS. This is part of the peripheral system and organizes internal goings-on by itself, subconsciously—only alerting the thinking, sentient level if something goes awry.

THE MASTER SWITCH

Working in concert with the brain and nerves is the second bodywide coordination–control–command system: hormonal or endocrine. It is based on natural chemicals called hormones, made in parts of the body known as endocrine glands. The two systems are integrated by a grape-sized area of the lower front brain, the hypothalamus, and the baked-beanlike pituitary gland dangling below it. So the executive director and chief operating officer are a tasty duo.

HYPOTHALAMUS

This has direct nerve connections to many other brain parts. It makes releasing factors (hypothalamic hormones) that tell the pituitary what to do and receives feedback from the pituitary. Its functions happen in groups of nerve cells called hypothalamic nuclei.

ANTERIOR

POSTERIOR

PITUITARY

This is controlled by the hypothalamus and pineal gland. It makes and/or releases hormones that control many other glands and processes (see next page). It also sends feedback to hypothalamus.

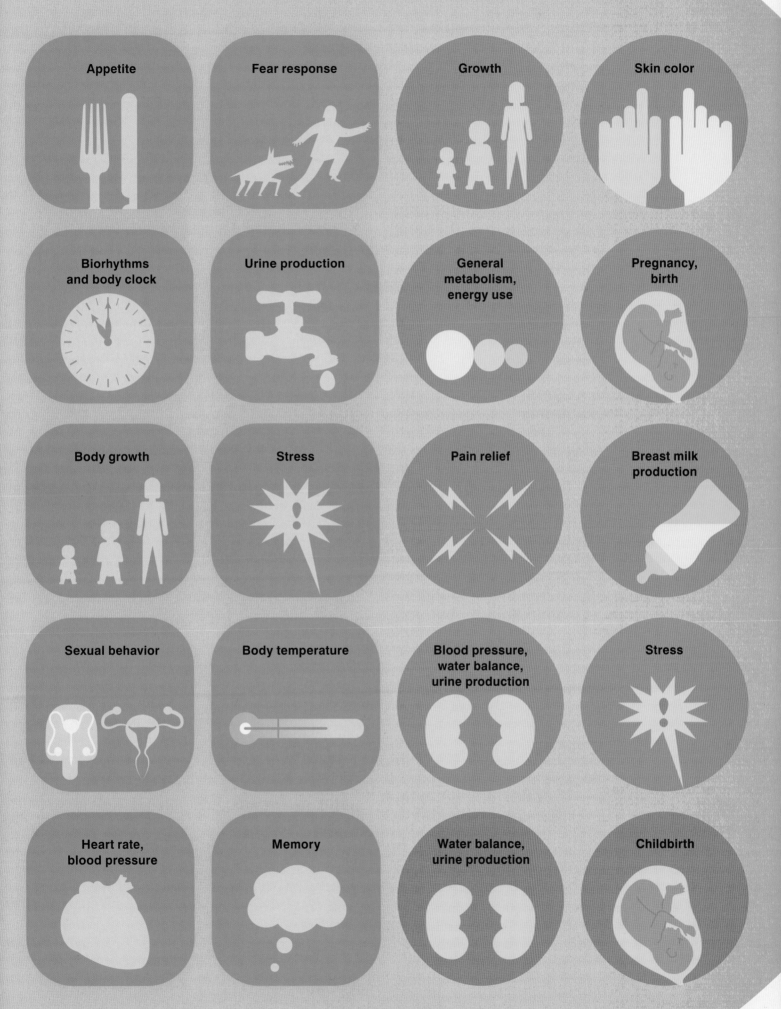

Appetite

Fear response

Growth

Skin color

Biorhythms and body clock

Urine production

General metabolism, energy use

Pregnancy, birth

Body growth

Stress

Pain relief

Breast milk production

Sexual behavior

Body temperature

Blood pressure, water balance, urine production

Stress

Heart rate, blood pressure

Memory

Water balance, urine production

Childbirth

CHEMICALS IN CONTROL

Blood is not only nourishing and a distributor. It is also the massive highway network for hormones to spread around the body. Each hormone is a small, blood-borne chemical substance. It comes from a particular endocrine gland, reaches every nook and cranny, but only affects certain tissues and organs, known as its targets.

PITUITARY
"Master gland" of the hormone system

Products
Ten-plus hormones and similar substances
(see previous page)

Targets
Most parts, from cells to large organs

Size
⅗ x ⅖ in

PINEAL
Regulates sleep-wake patterns, biorhythms

Products
Melatonin

Targets
Most parts, especially brain

Size
⅖ x ¼ in

THYROID
Regulates metabolism, speed of body processes;
controls blood calcium levels

Products
Thyroxine, triiodothyronine; calcitonin

Targets
Most cells of the body

Size
4 x 1⅛ in

PARATHYROIDS
Control blood calcium levels

Products
Parathyroid hormone

Targets
Most cells of the body

Size
¼ x ⅕ in

PANCREAS
Regulation of blood glucose (see next page)

Products
Insulin; glucagon

Targets
Most body cells

Size
5 x 1½ in

STOMACH
Release of acid and other digestive juices

Products
Gastrin; cholecystokinin; secretin

Targets
Stomach; pancreas, gall bladder; pancreas

Size
12 x 6 in

ADRENAL 1: OUTER (CORTEX)
Regulates water and mineral levels; responses to stress; sexual development, activity

Products
Aldosterone; cortisol; sex hormones

Targets
Kidney and gut; most body parts; sex organs

Size
Whole gland 2 x 1½ in

ADRENAL 2: INNER (MEDULLA)
Prepares body for action (fright, fight, flight)

Products
Adrenaline and similar hormones

Targets
Many body parts

Size
Whole gland 2 x 1⅕ in

THYMUS
Stimulates white cells to fight disease

Products
Thymosin and similar hormones

Targets
White blood cells

Size
2 x 2 in in childhood, shrinks in adult

KIDNEY
Water and mineral balance, blood pressure; red blood cell production

Products
Renin (an enzyme); erythropoietin

Targets
Kidney and blood circulation; bone marrow

Size
4⅗ x 2⅖ in

BREAKFAST

MIDDAY MEAL

HIGH

NORMAL

LOW

IN THE LOOP

Hormones need careful control. They circulate in the body in tiny amounts, often fractions of a gram, but their powers are great. For many hormones there is a push–pull system where one hormone raises the level of its target or makes a process speed up, while another—its agonist—has the opposite effect. Shown here is the story of blood glucose (sugar), the energy source that every body cell needs to stay alive and do its job, and how its levels are kept steady by two pancreatic hormones.

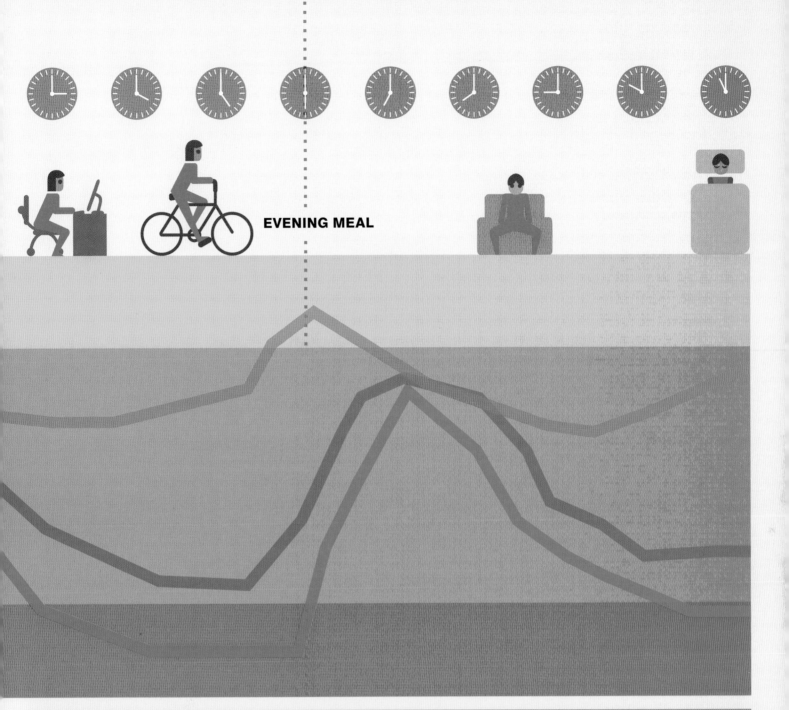

EVENING MEAL

GLUCAGON
Source: Alpha cells in the islets of the pancreas.

Function: Raises level of glucose in blood by telling the liver to convert glycogen (starch) into glucose.

Levels: Glucagon goes down when the others go up, and after more of a time lag, 1–2 hours.

BLOOD GLUCOSE
Source: Food and drinks, especially sugary and starchy ones (carbohydrates).

Function: Provides energy for metabolic processes in every cell.

Levels: Rise after food is eaten (especially with high-carb foods) and fall with activity and exercise.

INSULIN
Source: Beta cells in the islets of the pancreas.

Function: Lowers level of glucose in blood by encouraging its take-up by cells and its conversion into glycogen in the liver.

Levels: Insulin follows glucose, a few minutes after.

GOING STEADY

A balance of water and minerals is vital to good health. As the body eats, drinks, breathes, sweats, exercises, and does almost anything else, the balance is liable to become disturbed. Several parts and hormones work together to make sure this does not happen and preserve the status quo.

HYPOTHALAMUS
Senses levels of water and minerals in blood, makes some hormones, including ADH (antidiuretic hormone, also called vasopressin)

PITUITARY
Makes, stores, releases hormones, including ADH

Kidneys
Produce renin. Filter wastes from blood. Contain about a million microfilters called nephrons

Wastes, water, and minerals filtered out into tubule

Under hormone control (ADH, aldosterone, ANP) some water and minerals are taken back into blood, according to body's needs

Unfiltered blood flows through knot of capillaries

Urine out to bladder

LOW BLOOD PRESSURE

When levels of water in blood decrease and blood pressure falls

Pituitary gland releases ADH (antidiuretic hormone, or vasopressin)

BLOOD PRESSURE RISES

Renin released by kidneys converts AT1 (angiotensin 1) from liver to AT2

ADH targets kidneys to make them remove more water from urine into the blood

Narrower blood vessels and more water in blood

AT2 makes blood vessels narrower to raise blood pressure, and stimulates adrenal gland to release aldosterone

ADH also makes blood vessels narrower to raise blood pressure

Aldosterone targets kidneys so they remove more water from urine into blood

Targets kidneys to make them remove less water from urine

Less water from kidneys goes into blood so blood volume decreases

ANP (atrial natriuretic peptide) made in atria (upper chambers) of heart is released

BLOOD PRESSURE LOWERS

HIGH BLOOD PRESSURE

When levels of water in blood increase and blood vessels are narrowed

THINKING BODY

BRAIN BY NUMBERS

There is a wide range of sizes for normal brains (broad averages are shown here), and no simple link between these overall dimensions and intelligence. Despite the brain's still, inert appearance, it buzzes with nervous electrical and chemical activity, making it—on average—the most energy-hungry organ in the entire body.

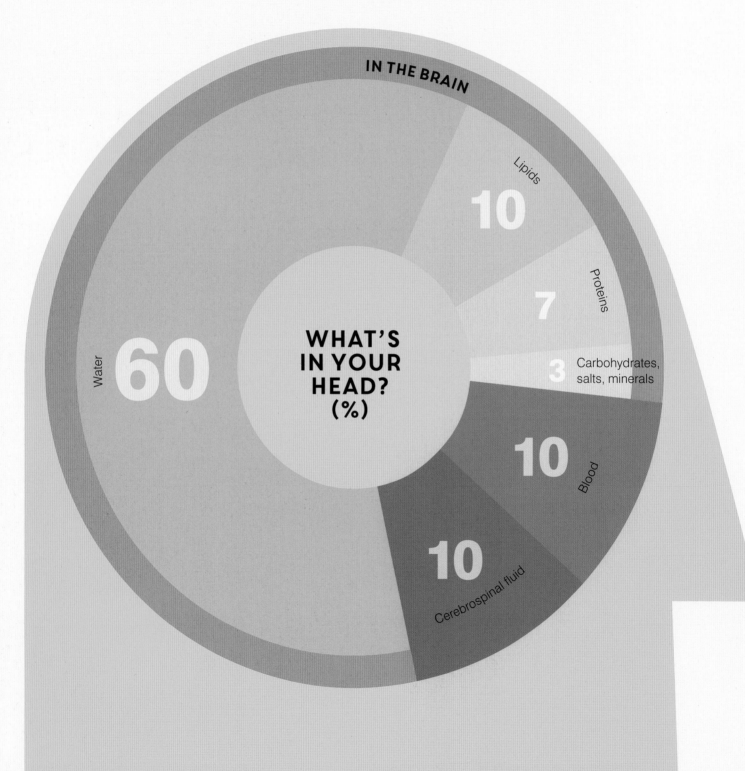

IN THE BRAIN

Lipids

10

Proteins

7

Carbohydrates, salts, minerals

3

Water

60

WHAT'S IN YOUR HEAD? (%)

Blood

10

Cerebrospinal fluid

10

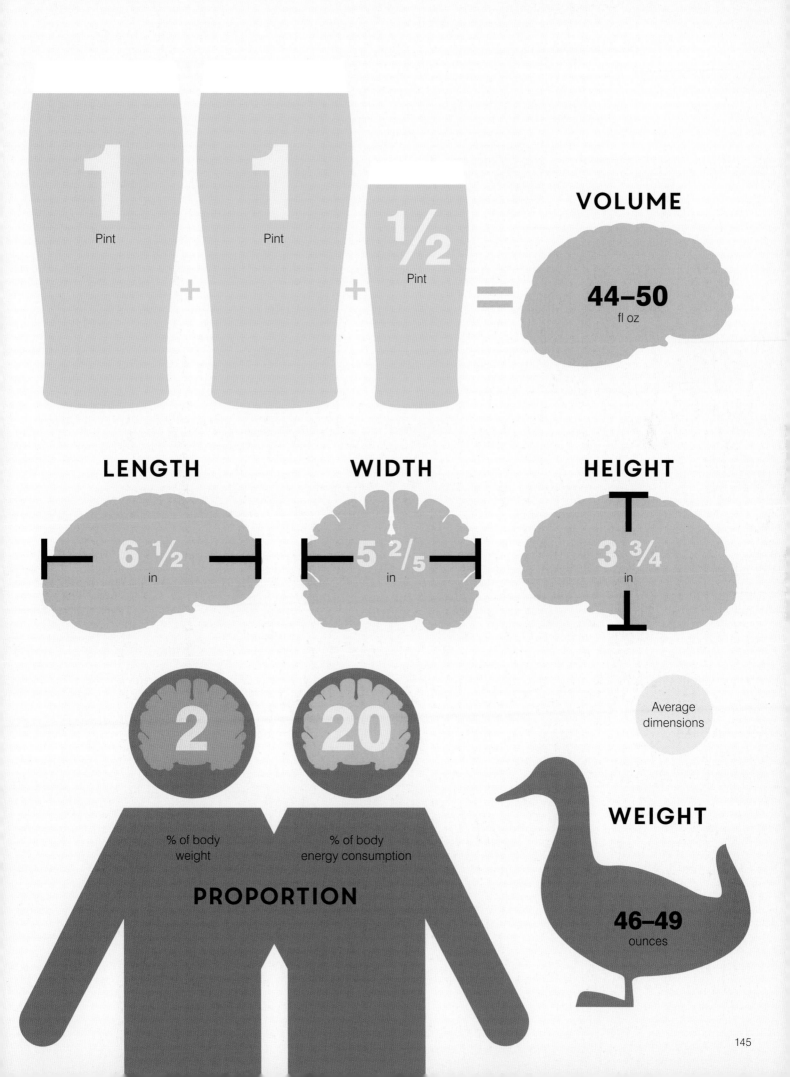

VOLUME

1 Pint + **1** Pint + **½** Pint = **44–50** fl oz

LENGTH

6 ½ in

WIDTH

5 ²/₅ in

HEIGHT

3 ¾ in

Average dimensions

2 % of body weight

20 % of body energy consumption

PROPORTION

WEIGHT

46–49 ounces

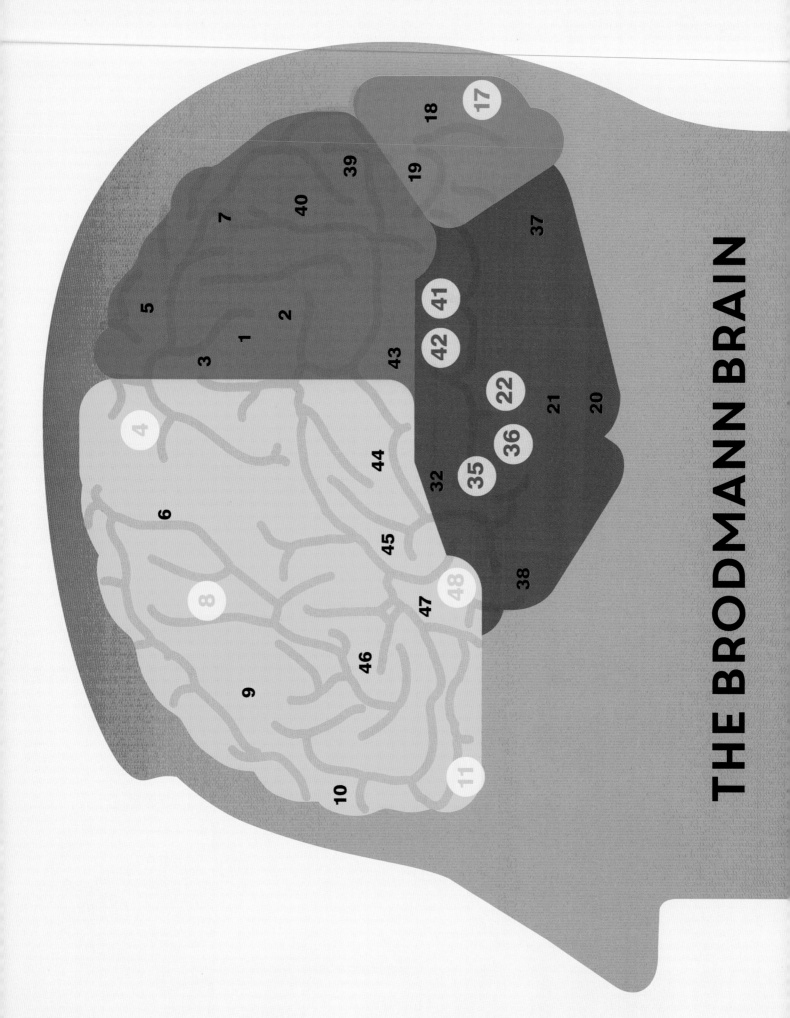

THE BRODMANN BRAIN

Look very, very closely at the cortex (the main folded surface of the brain). Its microscopic nerve cells are not all the same. Their shapes, numbers, sizes, and six-layered organization vary, like a patchwork. The patches are called Brodmann areas, and each has its own number and its own roles. A selection of the main areas and their function is shown here.

4 MOVEMENTS Primary motor cortex
Orders contractions of muscles to make movements.

8 DECISIONS Prefrontal cortex
Among several sites involved in doubts, decisions, and uncertainty.

11 REWARD Prefrontal cortex
Among several sites for making decisions, assessing rewards, reasoning, and long-term memory.

17 SIGHT Primary visual cortex
Main destination for messages from the eyes concerning vision.

22 SPEECH Understanding words
Wernicke's area (left side), ambiguity (right side).

35, 36 SIGHT & MEMORY Temporal cortex
Allows seen objects to be recognized and given meaning.

41, 42 HEARING Primary auditory cortex
Main destination for messages from the ears concerning sounds.

48 AWARENESS Prefrontal cortex
Among several sites for working memory, awareness, attention, and concentration.

Up to **100,000** strands

2–3

0.5–1

4–6

All measurments in mm and show thickness.

2–8

BRAIN CORTEX

ALL WRAPPED UP

The brain is the most precious body part—and it's well protected by lots of natural layers around it. These provide a delicate, intermeshed combination of strength, security, cushioning, and flexibility. The three main layers are the dura, arachnoid, and pia, collectively called the meninges. (One layer, singular, is a meninx.) Extras can be added on the outside, like a hard hat…

SUBDURAL SPACE

This is "potential space" since the dura is usually attached to the arachnoid, and the dura and arachnoid separate only with problems (disease, injury).

HAIR

These are keratin-based strands. Each strand self-renews after 3–5 years.

SCALP SKIN

Chiefly made up of collagen, elastin, and keratin proteins, it is self-renewing after 4 weeks.

PERIOSTEUM
Tough outer "skin" covering bone tissue.

SKULL BONE

The cranium of the skull, the part covering the brain, consists of eight cranial bones connected by firm, fused joints called sutures.

MENINGES 1: DURA MATER

Translated as "Tough Mother," this layer is a tough, strong outer casing for the other meninges and brain. It consists of dense fibers arranged in layers called laminae, and supports blood vessels and varied blood spaces (sinuses).

0.1–3

MENINGES 2: ARACHNOID MATER

The "Spider Mother" layer is a delicate spongy web of collagen and other connective tissue, and fluids. It is a flexible foamlike cushion that absorbs the impact of shocks to the head.

0.1

MENINGES 3: PIA MATER

The meshlike fiber network of the "Tender Mother" is the last line of protection against contact with the cortex, and closely follows the contours of the brain surface.

0.3–8 SUB-ARACHNOID SPACE

This contains cerebrospinal fluid and is a flowable, fluid cushion that absorbs impact shocks to head.

CUTAWAY BRAIN

It's not much to look at—a wrinkled lump of gray and white, with a few curved squiggly bits inside. Yet this is the control center for the physical body, the chief coordinator for the chemical body, the mental body's seat of the mind, the storehouse for memories, the origin of emotions, and the second-by-second hub for conscious awareness.

CEREBRUM
Large upper wrinkled dome divided into two hemispheres. Forms 80% of whole brain by volume.

Contents: Mostly white matter, nerve fibers (axons)

Function: Links cortex to rest of brain

CORPUS CALLOSUM
4 in-long connecting strap between left and right hemispheres

Contents: More than 200 million nerve fibers

Function: Lets each side of the body know what the other side is doing—literally

MIDBRAIN
Forms 10% of whole brain by volume

Contents: Mix of nerve cells and fibers

Function: Mainly concerned with automatic body maintenance

THALAMUS
Twinned egg-shaped lumps, 2–2⅖ in long

Contents: Nerve cells and fibers organized in areas called nuclei

Function: Gatekeeper to the cortex and conscious mind

CEREBRAL CORTEX
Thin gray covering of cerebrum
Contents: 20 billion nerve cells (neurons)
Function: Site of awareness and most conscious-thought processes

BRAIN STEM
Lowest part of the brain, merging into spinal cord below
Contents: Mix of nerve cells and fibers
Function: Site of centers for basic body processes such as breathing, heartbeat (see pages 128/132)

PONS
Size top–bottom ¾–1⅖ in
Contents: Mainly nerve fibers
Function: Link between lower and higher brain parts

CEREBELLUM OR LITTLE BRAIN
Forms 10% of whole brain by volume
Contents: 50-plus billion nerve fibers
Function: Involved in movement and coordination (see next page)

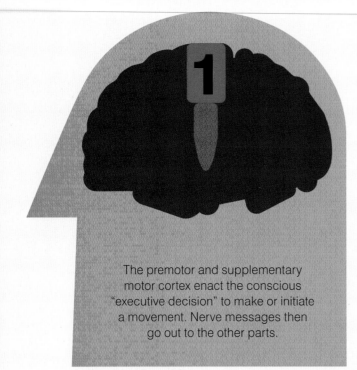

1

The premotor and supplementary motor cortex enact the conscious "executive decision" to make or initiate a movement. Nerve messages then go out to the other parts.

2

The primary motor cortex (movement center) has a striplike body map with more area devoted to parts that can be moved highly accurately and precisely, such as the fingers.

MAKE YOUR MOVE

Movements seem so simple. The brain thinks about them, and they happen. But the process involves several brain parts sending messages to and fro between them, especially strips on the surface called the motor cortexes, also the cerebellum at the rear, thalamus in the center, small parts deep in the brain called basal ganglia, and others. Then there's the journey from the brain along nerves to the muscles, to make them contract, which pulls the bone and makes them move. So overall, not quite that simple…

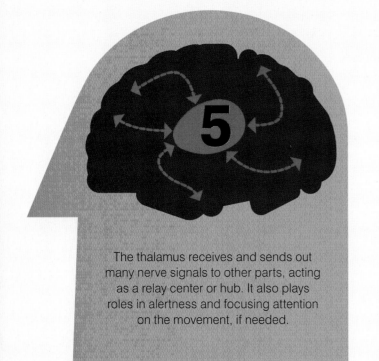

5

The thalamus receives and sends out many nerve signals to other parts, acting as a relay center or hub. It also plays roles in alertness and focusing attention on the movement, if needed.

6

The premotor cortex monitors information from the eyes, muscles, and joints about the progress of the movement, and makes small, ongoing adjustments as required.

3 The cerebellum synchronizes the numerous muscles involved in even the simplest movement, for example, ensuring one muscle relaxes when its partner contracts. This make actions smooth and coordinated.

4 The basal ganglia help to organize and coordinate the muscles involved, especially for habitual or routine movements whose instructions have been learned and stored.

8 Each nerve fiber ends at a series of spiderlike structures called nerve-muscle junctions (motor end plates). The electrical pulses of the nerve messages pass into the muscle and make it shorten.

7 Motor fibers snake out all over the body along nerves, direct to the muscles they control.

LEFT OR RIGHT?

The two sides of the brain look almost identical, but in the way they work and what they control, they are not the same. Some of these differences relate to whether a person is right- or left-handed. Some are linked to how the brain learns to do various tasks. And some differences are hardwired into the brain's nerve circuits. The general term for this is lateralization of brain function—although more and more research shows the differences are more complex than once thought.

13 August each year is Left-hander's Day

Selfish
Tends to interact with itself more than with the right hemisphere.

Talkative
Tends to dominate in language, vocabulary, syntax, grammar—especially in right-handed people.

Hard
Often said to take charge in analytical "hard" processes such as numerical tasks, calculations, formulae, logic, step-by-step reasoning, categorizing, definitions, efficiency, science, and technology.

BUT recent research shows this is less clear-cut than once thought

In most human communities, an average of **1 in 10 people is left-handed,** which means they preferentially use their left hand, especially for dexterous tasks and delicate manipulation. However, this average disguises a wide range, from 1 in 4 to 1 in 50.

Despite many myths to the contrary, there's little hard evidence to show that a higher proportion of artistic, musical, and generally creative people are left-handed.

Left-handers tend to perform manipulative tasks better with their right hands than right-handers do with their left hands.

1   2   3   4   5   6   7   8   9   10

Sharing
Tends to interact with itself and left hemisphere equally.

Expressive
Tends to dominate in speech articulation, rhythm, expression, intonation, stressed words.

Soft
Often said to take charge in imaginative "soft" aspects such as intuition, sensitivity, visualizing, artistic and musical creativity, spatial and three-dimensional matters, recognizing faces, spontaneity, and flexibility.

Broca's area

Broca's area is in the left hemisphere in 85–90% of right-handers and 60–70% of left-handers. It is highly involved in language as the "brain's scriptwriter." It helps to plan speech, selects and organizes words to say, and monitors sounds and articulation to make ongoing adjustments.

Wernicke's area

Wernicke's area is in the left hemisphere of 85–90% of right-handers and 60–70% of left-handers. It is also highly involved in language, especially comprehension of speech and written words. Close to the auditory cortex, or hearing center, it recognizes and gives meaning to words and phrases.

THE FLUID BRAIN

It's official: the brain is mostly mush. About 75% of this most vital organ is water, chiefly found in and between cells. Aside from the brain, almost all the other skull contents are water-based too. The main liquids here are blood and a curious substance unique to the nervous system known as CSF, cerebrospinal fluid, which circulates slowly through chambers called ventricles—because the brain is hollow!

CSF AND THE BRAIN ■ ■ BLOOD AND THE BRAIN

Volume in brain at any moment (fl oz)

5 **4**

CSF provides physical protection and cushioning; removes wastes; helps regulate blood pressure in the brain; and supplies some nutrients.

Origin: Choroid plexuses lining brain ventricles

Fate: Absorbed in subarachnoid space and by veins

Blood delivers oxygen, energy (glucose), nutrients, and minerals; removes wastes; distributes warmth; and fights infection.

Origin: Heart's left ventricle via internal carotid (80%) and vertebral (20%) arteries

Fate: Heart's right ventricle via jugular veins

24				**11**	
6		**10**	**4**		**9**
Brain ventricles	**Brain's sub-arachnoid space**	**In and around spinal cord**	**Arteries**	**Capillaries and brain tissue**	**Veins**

Measured in teaspoons

156

In the brain

1

Red blood cells

2

3

THE TRIPLE-B

The brain has special protection from nasties in the blood such as many kinds of germs and toxic chemicals. This is the blood-brain barrier, the triple-B. It is based on three differences between brain capillaries and ordinary capillaries around the rest of the body.

1 Between cells forming capillary wall
In the brain: No gap
Rest of body: Gaps

2 Capillary wall base membrane
In the brain: Continuous
Rest of body: Gaps

3 Protective cells around capillary
In the brain: Protective astrocyte cells
Rest of body: None

In the rest of the body

1

Cell body of capillary wall cell

Red blood cells

2

Surrounding tissues

IN-HEAD INTERNET

The brain's main microfeatures are nerve cells, or neurons—more than 100 billion of them. The cerebellum at the lower rear has the majority, and the cortex has some 20 billion. But they are not the brain's only kinds of cells. Nerve cells are so delicate and specialized that they need help and support, which they get from glial cells. Glial (meaning "glue") cells outnumber nerve cells by perhaps 20 to one, and they do a lot more than simply hold things together. Types of glial cell include astrocytes, oligodendrocytes, and microglial cells.

ASTROCYTES

These cells support nerve cells both physically and with energy, nutrients, and other needs; maintain and affect synapses; help the blood-brain barrier; and repair nerve and other glial cells.

OLIGODENDROCYTES

These cells make the fatty covering or myelin sheath of axons (see page 152); and support nerve cells physically and with nutrients.

250,000 million

MICROGLIAL CELLS

These are specialized "resident defenders." Like white blood cells, they scavenge for and remove invaders, damaged parts of brain cells, and other unwanted material.

Speedy!

Microglia are the fastest-moving cells in the brain (apart from those borne along in a flow, as in blood). They race along at 0.1 mm per hour. At this rate, they would take four days to cover 1 cm (⅖ in). Their extensions can lengthen or shorten twice as quickly.

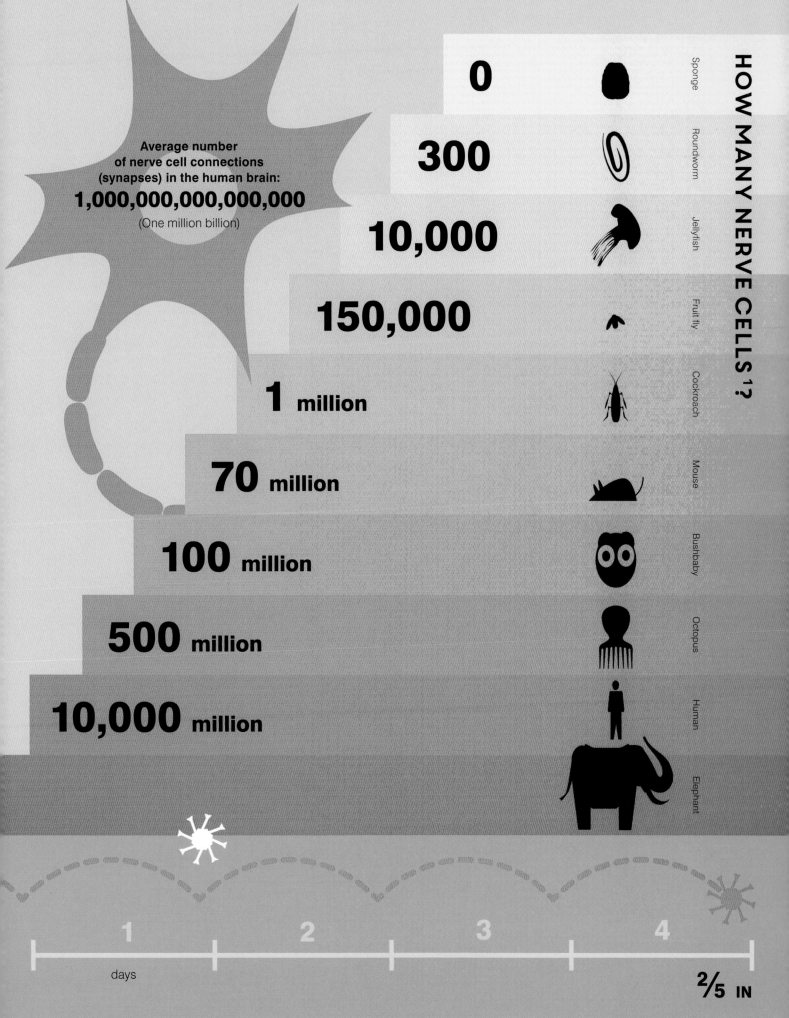

Average number
of nerve cell connections
(synapses) in the human brain:
1,000,000,000,000,000
(One million billion)

0	Sponge	
300	Roundworm	
10,000	Jellyfish	
150,000	Fruit fly	
1 million	Cockroach	
70 million	Mouse	
100 million	Bushbaby	
500 million	Octopus	
10,000 million	Human	
	Elephant	

1   2   3   4

days

2/5 IN

1 Neurons in the whole nervous system.

THE UNDERBRAIN

Beneath the great wrinkled dome of the right and left hemispheres, and in front of the "mini-brain" cerebellum, are the mid brain, brain stem, and other unfamiliar parts. They constantly work to keep the body's automatic systems running smoothly, to relay information between the consciously aware centers of the high brain and the rest of the body—as well as to carry out their own secretive, mysterious tasks.

Nucleus ruber (meaning "Red body")
Some automatic aspects of movement, such as swinging arms when walking and running.

Substantia nigra (meaning "Black stuff")
Part of mid brain. Planning and executing movements, head–eye movement coordination, pleasure, and reward-seeking and addictive behavior.

Tectum (meaning "Roof")
This part of the mid brain deals with processing sight and sound information and eye movement.

Pons (meaning "Bridge")
This link between lower and higher brain parts is involved in many and varied processes such as breathing, basic reflexes such as swallowing and urination, sight and other main senses, facial movements, sleep and dreams.

Cerebellum (meaning "Little brain")
Major hub for movement, balance, and coordination.

Medulla (meaning "Center, core")
Also called medulla oblongata, this merges below into the spinal cord, and is involved with many automatic (autonomic or involuntary) processes, actions and reflexes including heart rate, breathing rate, blood pressure, digestive activity, sneezing, coughing, swallowing, and vomiting.

BIG-HEADED

BIGGEST BRAIN

Bigger creatures, in general, have bigger brains, but they are not always cleverer, at least by our measures of intelligence. A sperm whale cannot play chess or memorize the Sun's planets. (But then, a human cannot hunt giant squid half a mile down in the ocean.) Measurements show weight in ounces.

Diplodocus **1:100,000**

Elephant
1:550

½
Rabbit

2
Kangaroo

4
Wolf

25
Giraffe

49
Human

175
Elephant

Horse
1:600

Cat
1:100

BIGGEST BRAINS FOR BODY SIZE

Comparing brain size to body size gives another measure that seems more linked to intelligence. Animals with larger ratios show features such as planning, problem-solving, and adapting behavior to novel situations. Ratio of brain mass to body mass.

Dolphin
1:100

Sparrow
1:15

Shark
1:2,500

Tree shrew
1:10

265

Sperm whale

Human
1:40

Ant
1:7

SENSES CROSSOVER

The brain normally processes the main senses separately. Sometimes, however, they get mixed or joined together. It can happen to anyone briefly, for example, a certain sound triggers a particular taste in the mouth, or a specific smell evokes mind–eye memories from long ago. In some people this sensory fusion is more common and known as synesthesia. Words have colors (even when printed black), shapes provoke tastes, certain kinds of touch stimulate sounds.

% SYNESTHETIC PEOPLE[1]
COMBINATION EXPERIENCED

15 Musical sounds provoke colors

20 Time units (hours, months) prompt colors

6 Colors stimulate smells

3 Sounds generate skin touch sensations

0.5 Smells have particular sounds

70 Letters, numbers, shapes trigger colors

[1] Some synesthetic people experience several kinds of combinations.

[2] These associations are representative, as experiences vary from person to person.

TASTE–SOUND COMBINATIONS[2]

In some cases of synesthesia, a sound can trigger a particular taste in the mouth.

SHOUT
Apple

WAIL
Plum

SOB
Lemon

HUM
Orange

SIGH
Cranberry

TUT
Banana

COLORED MONTHS[2]

In other cases, a month is associated with a color.

January   February   March   April

May   June   July   August

September   October   November   December

MEMORY BY NUMBERS

Memory is immense. The brain holds not only facts and information, like a friend's phone number or who wrote *On the Origin of Species*[1]. It also remembers faces, scenes, sounds, smells, touches on the skin, skills, and movement patterns such as writing and cycling, plus experienced emotions and feelings. There are over-simple comparisons for the storage capacity of brains and computers. Vital, too, are the size of "working memory" (in computers, RAM), and the speeds of storing and retrieving information.

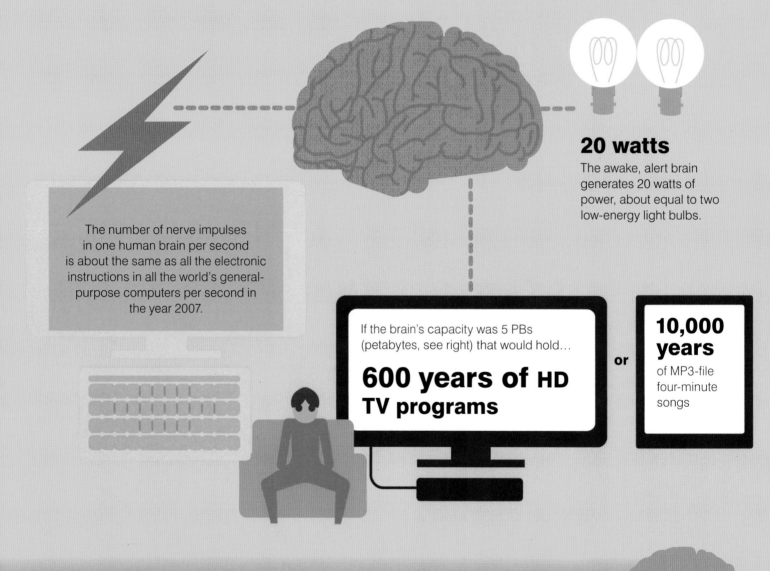

20 watts
The awake, alert brain generates 20 watts of power, about equal to two low-energy light bulbs.

The number of nerve impulses in one human brain per second is about the same as all the electronic instructions in all the world's general-purpose computers per second in the year 2007.

If the brain's capacity was 5 PBs (petabytes, see right) that would hold…

600 years of HD TV programs

or

10,000 years
of MP3-file four-minute songs

HOW FAST IS THE BRAIN?

One measure of computer processing speed or performance is FLOPS, floating point operations per second. A FLOP can be imagined as one calculation or computation. Assume:

- The brain has 100 million nerve cells.
- Each nerve cell connects to an average of 1,000 others.
- Each synapse, or connection between nerve cells, has about 20 different forms.
- Neurons fire up to 200 times per second.

Multiplied out, the brain's rate is 400 petaFLOPS (one million billion or one quadrillion FLOPS). This compares to supercomputer speeds of 10–50 PFLOPS.

1 Charles Darwin, book published 1859. Remember that.

HOW MUCH MEMORY?

Typical storage capacity of everyday working device:

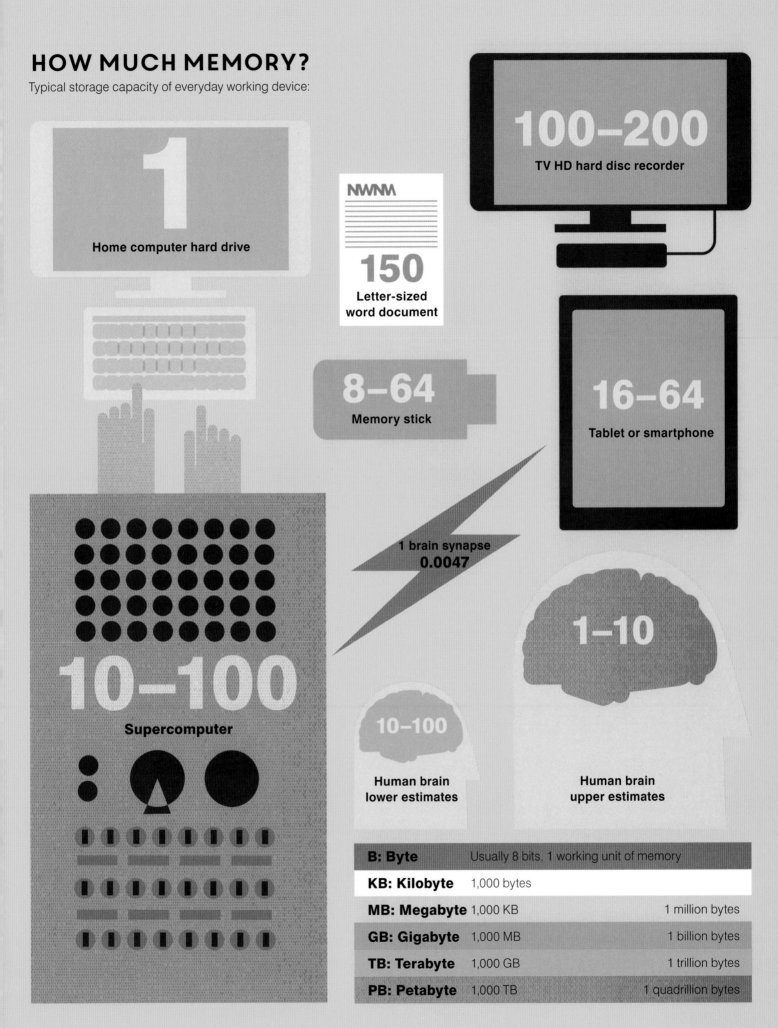

1
Home computer hard drive

NWNM

150
Letter-sized
word document

8–64
Memory stick

100–200
TV HD hard disc recorder

16–64
Tablet or smartphone

10–100
Supercomputer

1 brain synapse
0.0047

1–10

10–100

Human brain
lower estimates

Human brain
upper estimates

B: Byte	Usually 8 bits, 1 working unit of memory	
KB: Kilobyte	1,000 bytes	
MB: Megabyte	1,000 KB	1 million bytes
GB: Gigabyte	1,000 MB	1 billion bytes
TB: Terabyte	1,000 GB	1 trillion bytes
PB: Petabyte	1,000 TB	1 quadrillion bytes

THE MEMORY GAME

Perhaps inconveniently, the brain has no single memory center. Indeed, there is no single type of memory, but several kinds. Numerous brain parts handle different aspects of their learning, storage, and recall. These parts are also wired into other brain regions, including emotional areas. So, moods and emotional states, along with fatigue, hunger, distractions, and many other factors, greatly affect memory. At the level of cells, a memory is a new pattern of connections and pathways between the brain's billions of neurons.

A B C D

Declarative (explicit)
Needs awareness and conscious effort to recall.

Episodic—events (episodes) with places, times, other people, associated feelings and emotions.

Semantic—general knowledge, facts, concepts, meanings, usually explainable in words.

Procedural (implicit)
Recalled automatically, without consciously thinking about it, such as well-practiced movement patterns and thought processes.

Emotional
Memories with high emotional content, arousal, and strong feelings, which recur around the body when the memory is recalled.

Topographic (visual–spatial)
Awareness and memory of surroundings, recognizing and locating objects and scenes, navigating a route.

TYPES OF
MEMORY

Movement (motor) cortex
Holds movement memories (procedural)

Touch cortex
(Somatosensory)
Stores touch memories

Frontal lobes
Main site of short-term "working memory," such as topographic awareness. Hold much associative information linking to other regions for various elements of a memory.

Hearing cortex
Holds sound memories

Taste cortex
Holds flavor memories

Smell cortex
Stores odor memories

Amygdala
Major roles in forming memories with high content of emotions and feelings (emotional memory). Important roles in memory consolidation, converting short- to long-term memory (with hippocampus).

Hippocampus
Important roles in memory consolidation, converting short- to long-term memory (with amygdala). Involved in spatial memory of objects in surroundings and navigation (topographic memory).

Sight cortex
Stores visual memories

Cerebellum
Stores movement memories (procedural)

SHARING MEMORIES

Many brain parts hold different aspects or components of memory. For instance, the vision center, or cortex, holds the image-based information that allows an object to be recognized, named, and incorporated into a larger memory experience. Much combining of memory elements into conscious awareness happens in the frontal lobes.

EMOTIONAL BRAIN

"Is that true? Oh no, how awful. Tragedy!" The body responds with faintness, trembling, unsteadiness, perhaps sobbing. The mood is distraught, the mind cannot think straight or make sensible decisions. "No, wait—it's not true. Fantastic!" Spirits rise, the body jumps for joy. Cries of anguish turn to delight, and tears of pleasure replace those of pain. Where in the brain do such powerful emotions come from?

Depression Happiness Sadness Surprise Anxiety

THE LIMBIC SYSTEM

This system is defined by function, that is, parts that contribute to feelings, moods, and emotions. (The parts have various other tasks too.)

Hippocampus
Forms and exports long-term memories (but does not store them itself). With the amygdala, helps in emotional components of memory and their recall.

Amygdala
Highly active (with hippocampus) in processing memories and their recall. Especially involved in emotions—minute by minute, recalled, and even imagined.

Olfactory bulb
Sends smell messages direct to amygdala, hippocampus, and other limbic parts. This is why odors and perfumes evoke such strong, immediate emotions and forceful memories.

WHERE ARE EMOTIONS FELT?

Each person has subjective feelings for which parts of the body are affected by strong emotional states. The feelings can be mapped onto a body outline.

Strong, hot, fast, positive

Neutral

Weak, cold, slow, negative

+

-

Shame

Anger

Pride

Fear

Love

Fornix
Intermediary between hippocampus, thalamus, and mammillary bodies. Contributes to emotional aspects of memory.

Parahippocampal gyrus
Memory and recognition of whole scenes (rather than people, objects in them) and emotional responses to these.

Mamillary bodies
Involved in episodic memories, those dealing with events (episodes): places, times, people, feelings.

Hypothalamus
Tends to be involved in bodily expression of emotions rather than generating or originating them. Linked with emotional states such as disgust, displeasure, and uncontrollable laughter and tears.

Thalamus
Relay station and distribution center for other limbic parts.

Limbic area of frontal lobe
Front, lower, inward-facing region of the brain surface. Major hub and association area for many kinds of memory, including spatial awareness and navigation. Transfer area between hippocampus and its linked areas, and the rest of the cortex.

BRAIN TIME

The body has its own built-in biological clock, the SCN, suprachiasmatic nucleus. Its nerve cells have a 24-hour or circadian ("about one day") activity cycle of their own—well, approximately. This activity is synchronized or entrained to the outside world by the natural daylight–darkness sequence detected by the eyes, which "sets" the clock. The SCN controls and coordinates biorhythms across the board, from body temperature and hormone levels, to appetite, digestion, waste removal, and the wake–sleep cycle.

SCN   Pineal gland

Clock-setting: 1
Daylight time is the primary environmental signal. Light levels are detected by ganglion cells in the retina of the eye, which send messages almost directly to the SCN. Other cues are shown opposite.

10–11PM

10–11PM

Sleep till 6–7am

Urine production and bowel activity slow

9–10PM

Blood pressure falls fastest

6–7PM

Highest body temperature and blood pressure

99.5°F

4–5PM

Greatest heart rate, muscle power, and stamina

3–4PM

Fastest reaction times

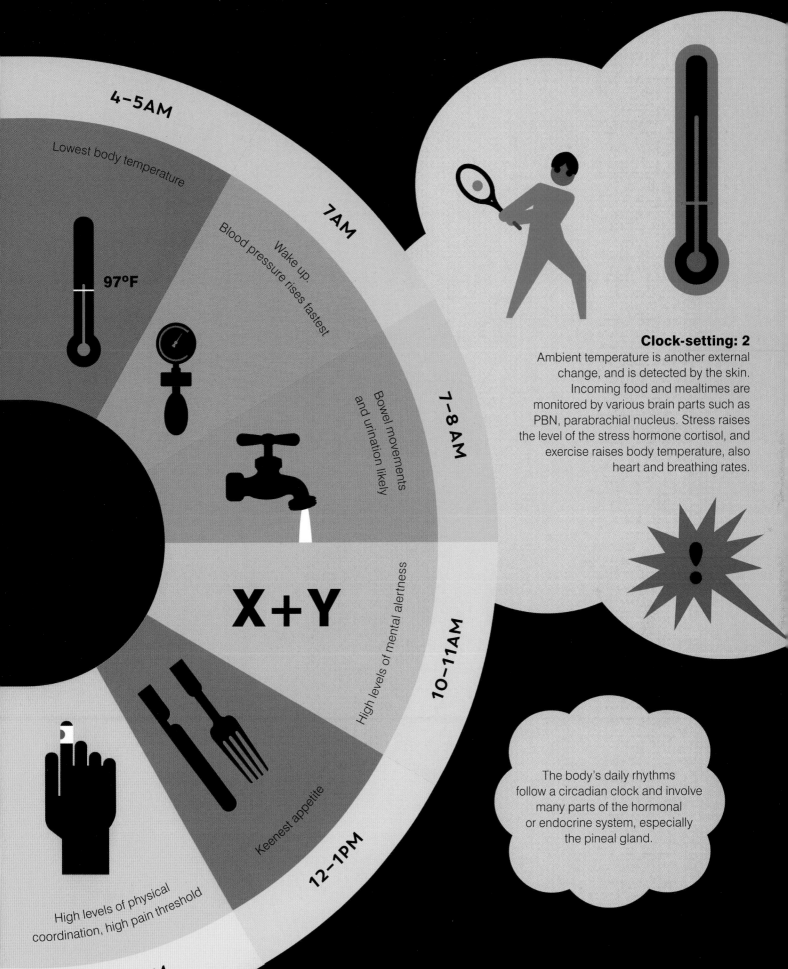

4–5AM

Lowest body temperature

97°F

7AM

Wake up.
Blood pressure rises fastest

Bowel movements
and urination likely

7–8 AM

X+Y

High levels of mental alertness

10–11AM

Keenest appetite

12–1PM

High levels of physical
coordination, high pain threshold

2–3PM

Clock-setting: 2
Ambient temperature is another external
change, and is detected by the skin.
Incoming food and mealtimes are
monitored by various brain parts such as
PBN, parabrachial nucleus. Stress raises
the level of the stress hormone cortisol, and
exercise raises body temperature, also
heart and breathing rates.

The body's daily rhythms
follow a circadian clock and involve
many parts of the hormonal
or endocrine system, especially
the pineal gland.

OFF TO SLEEP

Consolidating important and well-used memories, and discarding insignificant and little-used memories

Energy use and general metabolism

Wound healing

Tissue maintenance and repair

Intestines and digestive activity

Heart rate and blood pressure

"Rewiring" nerve cell connections throughout brain to reinforce learning

Cortex activity in brain

Breathing rate

Kidneys and urine production

Immune system activity

Speeds up

Slows down

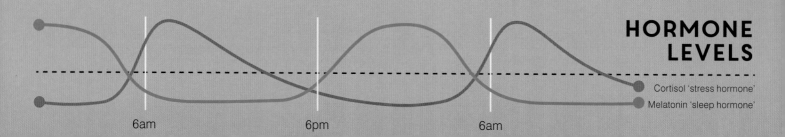

HORMONE LEVELS

Cortisol 'stress hormone'

Melatonin 'sleep hormone'

6am   6pm   6am

We spend one-third of our lives asleep, mainly due to melatonin from the brain's pineal gland. Sleep happens in stages from light or shallow to deep, plus a renegade stage called REM, when dreams happen. EEGs, electroencephalograms, are recordings of the brain's electrical activity, tracking the numbers, locations, and patterns of nerve signals. Each sleep stage and major mental process has a characteristic EEG trace. Through all this, the brain certainly does not rest; it's especially busy processing memories. Subsistence organs like the heart, lungs, guts, and kidneys take it easy. The immune and tissue-maintenance systems up their game and rush ahead with their tasks.

STAGES OF SLEEP

1 Light

Body: Muscles may twitch, especially eyes, face, limbs

Brain EEG: Theta wave

5-10

2 Medium

Body: Gradually increasing relaxation and stillness

Brain EEG: Sleep spindles, K complexes

45-50

3 Deep

Body: All activity and movements at lowest levels

Brain EEG: Delta waves (slow wave sleep)

15–25

4 REM

Body: Eyes move rapidly under closed lids, body activity and movements are erratic, e.g., twitching

Brain EEG: Alpha and theta waves

15–20

 % total sleep time
(In adults; amounts increase for younger ages)

NEED FOR REM SLEEP

Sleep needs vary hugely between individuals.
Sufficient REM sleep is especially important for good health.

| 50 | 30 | 20 | 15 |
| 70 | 40 | 25 | 15 |

| 14-17 | 12-15 | 11-14 | 10-13 | 9-11 | 8-10 | 7-9 | 7-8 |
| Newborn | Up to 1 | 1–2 | 3–5 | 6–13 | 14–17 | 18–64 | 65+ |

DREAMTIME

When people are wired up for EEGs and other body functions during sleep testing, and then woken up during REM, they usually report that they have been dreaming. Dreams can be reassuring, peculiar, unsettling, or truly nightmarish. EEGs and scans reveal which parts of the brain are engaged. However, the serious science of interpreting dreams has a long way to go.

Recommended hours of sleep per night[1]

 Proportion of REM sleep %

1 Guidelines from US National Sleep Foundation

WHERE'S BUSY DURING SLEEP?

Sleepy teens
It's official: adolescents really do find it difficult to get up in the morning. Research shows the body clock and daily biorhythms tend to run one or two hours later during the teenage years.

QUIET

1	**Motor (movement) center**
2	**Touch center**
3	**Primary visual (sight) center**
4	**Hearing center**
5	**Frontal lobe:** dampens conscious inputs

ACTIVE

6	**Smell center:** strong odors may wake dreamer
7	**Associated visual areas:** dream imagery
8	**Thalamus:** filters many sensory inputs to cortex
9	**Amygdala:** memory links to emotions
10	**Hippocampus:** short-term in-dream memory loss
11	**Medulla:** basic life maintenance

GROWING BODY

PRE-BABY PREP

A rule of life is: "All cells come from other cells" by division, or mitosis. A new life is the same, but with complications. Each cell in the body has a double set of genetic material. Babies are made from an egg cell and a sperm cell. If these two had a double set each, the result would be a quadruple set. So the double set must be halved to single, then sperm and egg fuse to make a twin set, to start the new baby. This is where a special kind of cell division comes in—meiosis, to make eggs and sperm.

GAMETE FORMATION IN THE MALE

Interphase

DNA forming pairs of chromosomes replicates. Result is two sets of 23 pairs of chromosomes.

Prophase/Metaphase 1

Chromosomes become visible. Some chromosomes may swap sections with their partners (crossing over) to introduce genetic variation. Nuclear membrane disintegrates. Chromosomes align at center or equator of cell.

Anaphase/Telophase 1

Pairs of chromosomes separate, one pair into each new cell. Nuclear membrane reforms in each sibling cell. Original cell has divided into two, each with a pair of each chromosome

GAMETE FORMATION IN THE FEMALE

The male gamete is called a sperm and contains 23 chromosomes, half the number needed for the formation of a zygote, the first cell of a new individual.

The female gamete is called an ovum (or egg) and contains 23 chromosomes, half the number needed for the formation of a zygote, the first cell of a new individual.

Prophase/Metaphase 2

Nuclear membrane disintegrates. Chromosomes align randomly at center or equator of cell.

Anaphase/Telophase 2

Chromosome pair separates, one into each new cell. Nuclear membrane reforms in each sibling cell.

Original cell has divided into four, each with only one of each chromosome.

One original male cell produces four sperm cells. One original female cell produces one egg cell plus three polar bodies (containing "spare" chromosomes).

MAKING EGGS

When the two sex cells—egg and sperm—join to start a new baby, they contribute an equal share of genes. Each has 23 chromosomes, each chromosome made of one length of DNA. However, production of mature sex cells is very unequal. In the female it begins around puberty, occurs about once every 28 days during the monthly cycle, and halts at the menopause. Sperm production, in great contrast, is a 24/7 process and fades gradually with age.

6–7
MILLION
present in
20-week fetus

1–2
MILLION
present at birth

350
THOUSAND
present at
puberty

1
THOUSAND
lost per month
from puberty to
menopause

1
mature egg
released
per month

450
mature eggs
released in
a lifetime

Average mature
20
mm
follicle size

Average egg cell
0.12
mm
diameter

REPRODUCTIVE CYCLE

The female reproductive cycle is coordinated by several hormones including FSH, LH, estrogen, and progesterone

Days	7	14	21	28

Body temperature
97.5
98

Egg
Primary follicle
Mature follicle
Egg released at ovulation
Corpus luteum
Corpus albicans

Hormone levels
FSH   Estrogen   LH   Progesterone

Uterus lining
Breaks down and expels
Grows in thickness

182

MAKING SPERM

Production of male sex cells, sperm, is a continuing process and happens in vast numbers, with millions daily growing and maturing within the testes. The production line begins around puberty, then continues every minute of every day, until it gradually tapers off with old age. However, men into their 70s and 80s have still fathered children in the natural way.

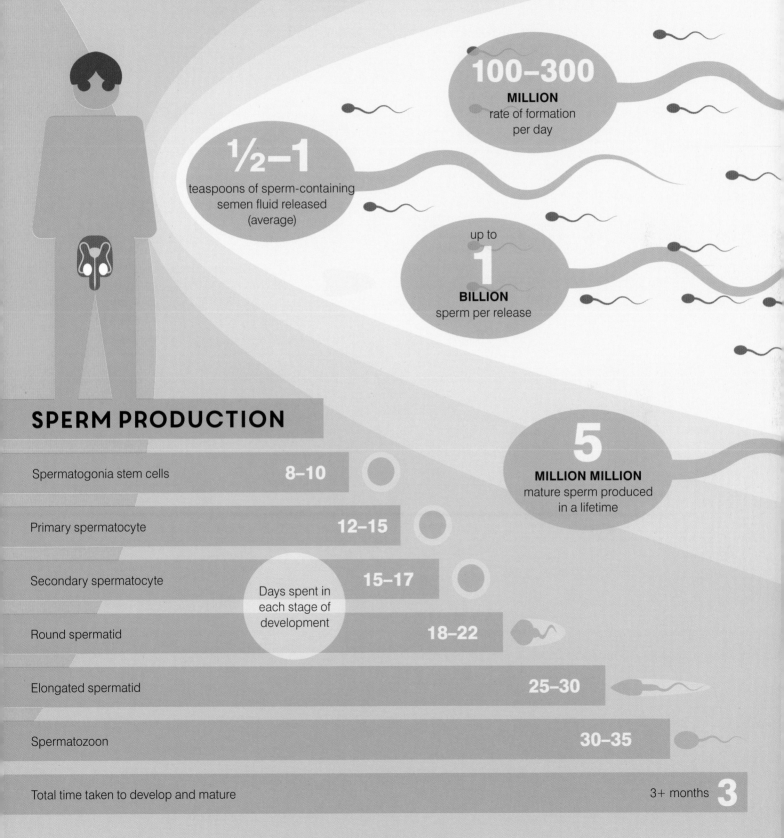

100–300
MILLION
rate of formation
per day

½–1
teaspoons of sperm-containing
semen fluid released
(average)

up to
1
BILLION
sperm per release

5
MILLION MILLION
mature sperm produced
in a lifetime

SPERM PRODUCTION

	Days spent in each stage of development	
Spermatogonia stem cells	8–10	
Primary spermatocyte	12–15	
Secondary spermatocyte	15–17	
Round spermatid	18–22	
Elongated spermatid	25–30	
Spermatozoon	30–35	
Total time taken to develop and mature	3+ months	**3**

NEW BODY BEGINS

The joining of egg and sperm cells to start a new baby is known as fertilization, and also conception, even syngamy. It usually happens in the oviduct (fallopian tube) leading from the ovary, where the egg came from, to the uterus (womb), where the baby will develop. The successful sperm is not just one in a million, but perhaps one in a billion. Nearly all of its fellows fail to reach the egg, and once it does make egg contact, the egg stops any more sperm joining. The joining of sperm and egg at conception sets off an amazing process of growth and development that, nine months later, results in a wrinkly, wailing, small human.

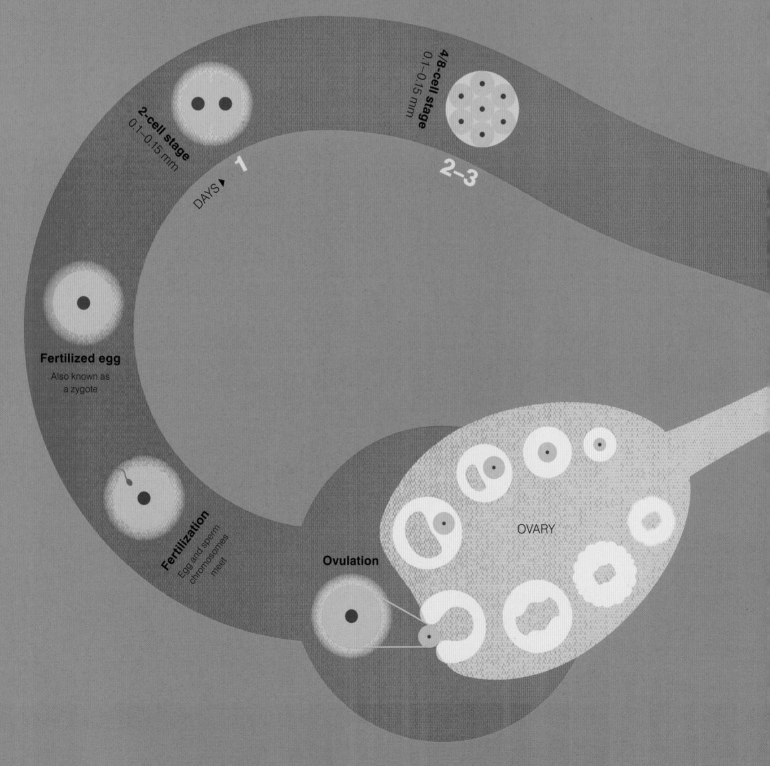

4/8-cell stage
0.1–0.15 mm

2-cell stage
0.1–0.15 mm

DAYS ▶ **1**

2–3

Fertilized egg

Also known as
a zygote

Fertilization
Egg and sperm
chromosomes
meet

Ovulation

OVARY

STAGES OF FERTILIZATION

1 Only a few hundred sperm reach the egg

2 Many sperm try to make contact

3 Cap (acrosome) releases enzymes to dissolve zona and egg outer membrane

4 One sperm head fuses with egg outer membrane

5 Sperm chromosomes in nucleus pass into egg

6 Zona and outer membrane toughen to prevent more sperm fusing

7 Sperm and egg chromosomes gather together; fertilized egg prepares for first division

Morula 0.1–0.15 mm

3–4

Blastocyst 0.2–0.3 mm

4–5

8–9

Implantation of blastocyst
Outer cells of blastocyst eat their way into uterus lining

21

Early embryo
First signs of brain, heart, and blood vessels

ACTUAL SIZE
2 mm

PREGNANCY TIMELINE

The baby grows in its very special place, the uterus. But it's not all calm, peace, and serenity. The mother's heartbeats thud above, and her blood whooshes through nearby arteries. Bright lights filter through the skin and uterus wall. So do sudden loud noises that can startle the baby so it punches or kicks. Increasing size means the baby becomes more cramped, and it is squeezed and squashed as the mother moves around.

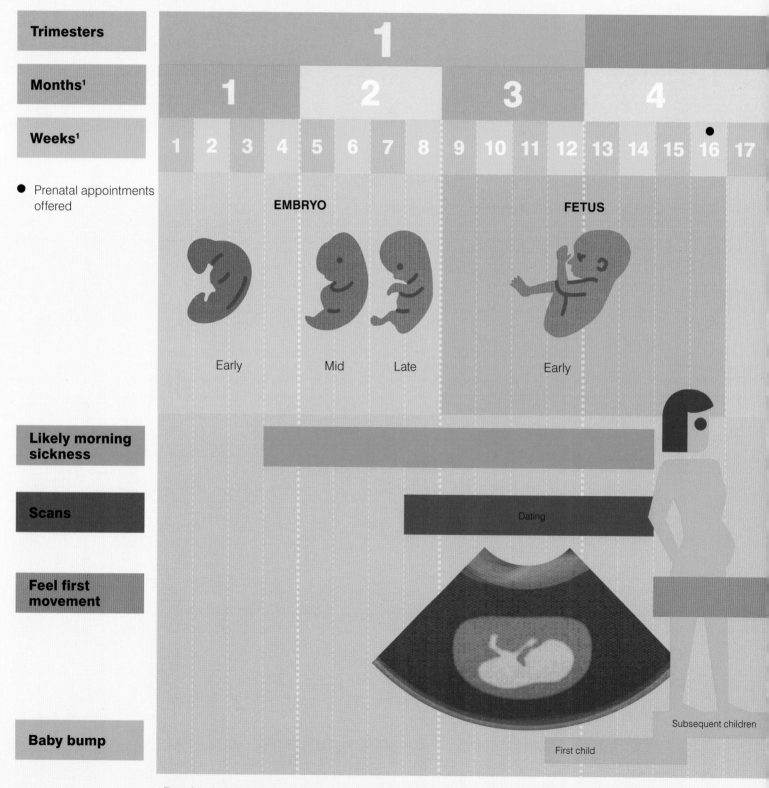

Trimesters: 1

Months[1]: 1, 2, 3, 4

Weeks[1]: 1 2 3 4 5 6 7 8 9 10 11 12 13 14 15 16 17

● Prenatal appointments offered

EMBRYO

Early — Mid — Late

FETUS

Early

Likely morning sickness

Scans — Dating

Feel first movement

Baby bump

Subsequent children

First child

1 Times from fertilization of egg by sperm, or conception. Some timelines are taken from the date of the mother's last menstrual period two weeks earlier, giving a total of 40 weeks.

PREGNANCY TEST ACCURACY

Tests detect the hormone hCG in the mother's urine, produced about 6 days after conception.

Accuracy, %		60		90	97
Days after conception			10	14	18

2

3

5 **6** **7** **8** **9**

| 18 | 19 | 20 | 21 | 22 | 23 | 24 | 25 | 26 | 27 | 28 | 29 | 30 | 31 | 32 | 33 | 34 | 35 | 36 | 37 | 38 |

FETUS

Mid

Viable[2]

Anomaly

2 Viability and perinatal period are defined in different ways by different authorities depending on, for example, improvements in newborn care and the proportion of babies likely to survive at a certain stage of development.

187

THE UNBORN BABY

Multiply, move, specialize: it happens every minute of the nine months before birth. The hundreds of cells in the embryo multiply to become thousands, then millions. They also physically move or migrate, forming folds, lumps, and sheets that gradually shape the organs. And they differentiate, that is, they change from the general, all-purpose stem cells of the early stages into particular different kinds such as bone, muscle, nerve, and blood cells.

4

• Heart beats 120–140 times per minute •

• Eye spots on head •

• Muscles forming, some movements occur •

• Arm buds appear •

• Tail present •

1/5 in

9 1/5 in

24

• Heart beats 150 times per minute •

• Head is one-quarter total length •

• Eyes can open •

• Thumb-sucking may occur •

• Early memories may form •

8

- Facial features recognizable -
- Head as big as body -
- Fingers and toes forming -
- Tail shrinks -
- Name changes from embryo to fetus -

3/5 in

16

- Face recognizably human -
- All organs formed -
- Milk teeth buds present in jaws -
- All bones shapes present, although mostly as cartilage -
- Fat starts to accumulate under skin -

2²/5 in

17³/4–19 in

36

- Lanugo (downy first hair) is shed -
- Nails may extend beyond fingers and toes -
- Coughs and hiccups common -
- Baby is ready for birth -
- Weight 6½ lb -

1 Times from fertilization of egg by sperm, or conception. Some timelines are taken from the date of the mother's last menstrual period two weeks earlier, giving a total of 40 weeks.

2 Because it is usually curled in the feta' position, embryo/fetus length is usually crown–rump, from top of head to base of bottom.

BIRTH DAY

Time taken to give birth famously varies from less than an hour to 24-plus hours; it usually reduces by 30–40% for second babies, and perhaps another 10–20% thereafter. Birth statistics in developed nations are being impacted by more assisted, intervened, and managed deliveries, especially induced labor and C-section (cesarean delivery). This means fewer babies are now born on Sunday than any other weekday, and the date with least births is often 25 December.

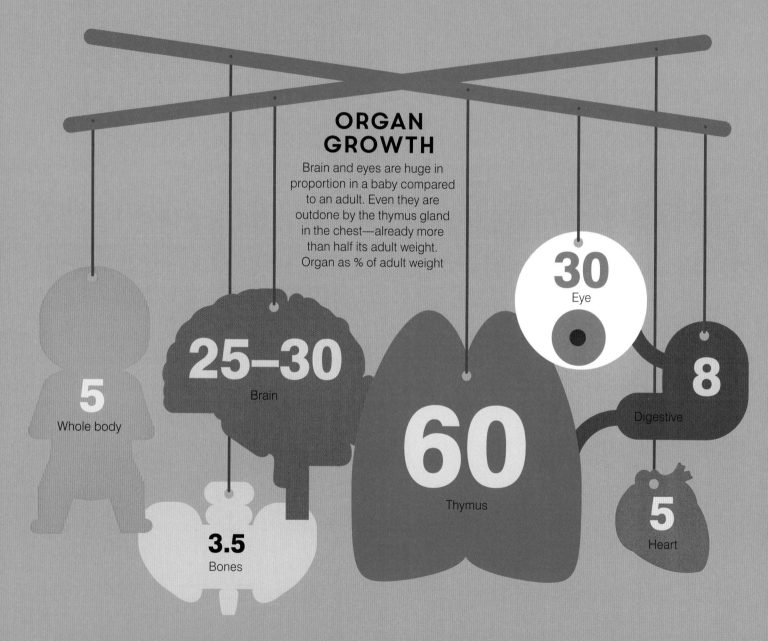

ORGAN GROWTH

Brain and eyes are huge in proportion in a baby compared to an adult. Even they are outdone by the thymus gland in the chest—already more than half its adult weight. Organ as % of adult weight

5
Whole body

25–30
Brain

3.5
Bones

60
Thymus

30
Eye

8
Digestive

5
Heart

TIMETABLE OF BIRTH, FIRST-TIME MOTHERS

Overall average 12–14 hours. Second and subsequent births are usually shorter, 6–8 hours.

Stages

1

Time in hours: **6–8**

Phase 1: Early Uterine contractions steadily increase in strength and frequency

Phase 2: Active

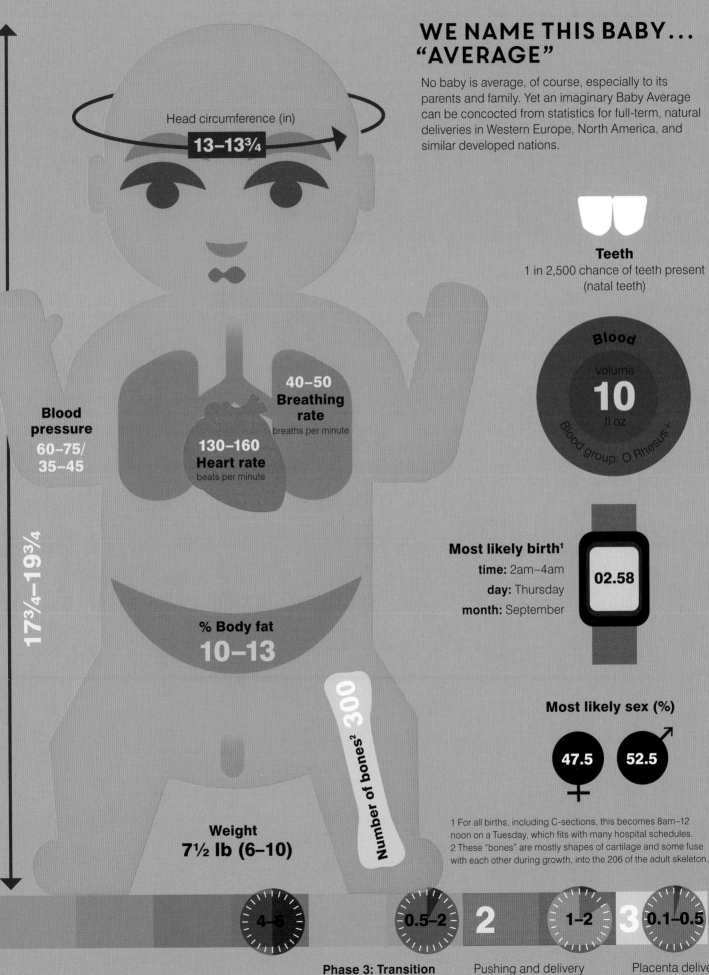

WE NAME THIS BABY... "AVERAGE"

No baby is average, of course, especially to its parents and family. Yet an imaginary Baby Average can be concocted from statistics for full-term, natural deliveries in Western Europe, North America, and similar developed nations.

Head circumference (in)
13–13¾

Teeth
1 in 2,500 chance of teeth present (natal teeth)

Blood
volume
10
fl oz
Blood group: O Rhesus-x

Blood pressure
60–75/
35–45

40–50 Breathing rate
breaths per minute

130–160 Heart rate
beats per minute

17¾–19¾

% Body fat
10–13

Number of bones[2] 300

Most likely birth[1]
time: 2am–4am
day: Thursday
month: September

02.58

Most likely sex (%)

47.5 ♀   52.5 ♂

**Weight
7½ lb (6–10)**

1 For all births, including C-sections, this becomes 8am–12 noon on a Tuesday, which fits with many hospital schedules.
2 These "bones" are mostly shapes of cartilage and some fuse with each other during growth, into the 206 of the adult skeleton.

4–6   0.5–2   2   1–2   3   0.1–0.5

Phase 3: Transition   Pushing and delivery   Placenta delivery

191

BABY TO CHILD

Each baby and child grows and develops at its own rate. Reaching one ability or skill early is not an accurate indicator of attaining others early, or eventual levels of ability. Some slow starters race ahead in later years, and vice versa. Others progress erratically. "Milestone" times can be useful to pick up the occasional worry. Reassuringly, the vast majority of children get there eventually.

15

- Vocabulary increases to 4–8 words
- Plays with ball
- Draws random simple lines
- May walk backward with aid

12

- Imitates movements of others
- Indicates wanting with gestures
- Says a few extra words
- Walks a few steps

18

- "Reads" books alone
- Begins to combine words into phrases
- Scribbles expressively
- Builds simple toy brick towers

21

DOG

- Walks up steps supervised
- Names cat, dog, etc. from pictures
- Kicks a ball
- Makes short 2–3 word phrases

5

- Hops, maybe skips, swings, climbs
- Speaks full sentences with varied verbs, e.g., future and past, singular and plural
- Copies simple shapes like circle, triangle

2

- Vocalizes gurgles, coos
- Holds head up for short periods
- Eyes follow moving objects
- Smiles responsively

 Months

4

- Coos in response to talking
- Holds head up for longer periods
- Bears weight on legs
- Grasps an object

9

 mama

- Combines syllables into wordlike sounds
- Stands when holding onto support
- Bangs, drops, and throws objects
- May mouth "mama"-type sounds

6

- Turns head toward sounds
- Rolls over in both directions
- Reaches for and mouths objects
- Sits without support

2

me me me

- Names body parts on dolls, animal toys
- Starts talking about self
- Arranges items in categories
- May start to jump

2.5

- Brushes teeth with help
- Draws lines at deliberate angles
- Puts on easyfit clothing
- Balances briefly on one foot

Years

4

 1 2 3 4

- Understands the basics of counting
- Catches a ball much of the time
- Breaks or cuts and eats own food
- Starts to copy letters when drawing

3

- Balances on one foot for several seconds
- Combines 4–6 words into sentences
- Names actions such as skip, jump, roll
- Potty-trained during day

GROWING UP

It's an amazing journey, from babyhood and infancy to child, teenager, and young adult. From birth, the body increases its height between three and four times, and its weight by 20 times or more. But the relative sizes of body parts at birth are far from their adult proportions, and their growth rates vary too.

GROWTH RATE CHARTS

A child on the 50th percentile means half of 100 children of the same age will be taller or heavier, and half shorter or lighter. Similarly for the 90th percentile, 10 will be taller or heavier, and 90 shorter or lighter.

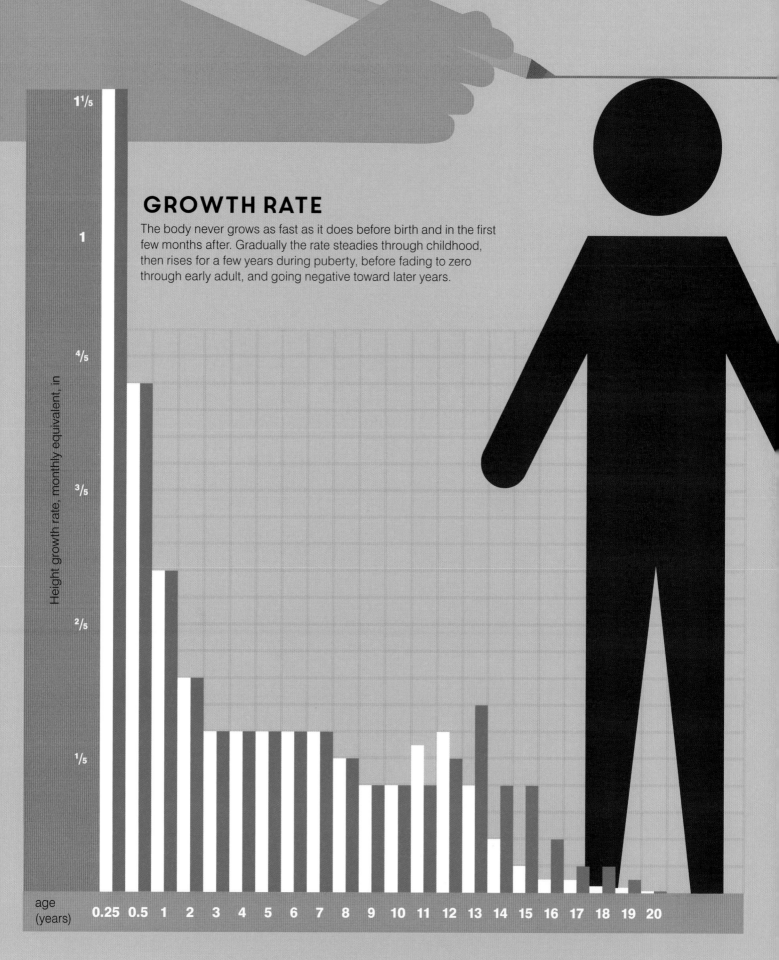

GROWTH RATE

The body never grows as fast as it does before birth and in the first few months after. Gradually the rate steadies through childhood, then rises for a few years during puberty, before fading to zero through early adult, and going negative toward later years.

Height growth rate, monthly equivalent, in

$1^1/_5$
1
$^4/_5$
$^3/_5$
$^2/_5$
$^1/_5$

age (years) 0.25 0.5 1 2 3 4 5 6 7 8 9 10 11 12 13 14 15 16 17 18 19 20

195

HOW LONG DO HUMANS LIVE?

Life expectancies are complicated. Some give a snapshot of estimated longevity in the general population at a certain time. Others categorize by sex and age, so women are expected to live longer than men, and estimated lifespans vary from young to old. Still others give projections for babies born on a specific date—any date. In general, all of these are getting longer. Of course, hugely important, too, are where people live, their health history, and—very significantly—their wealth.

79

NORTH AMERICA

79

WORLDWIDE AVERAGE LIFE EXPECTANCY IN YEARS

Girl born today

73

Woman aged 60 today

82

Apparent increase is due to surviving infancy and childhood, when mortality takes a significant toll, especially in less developed regions.

Boy born today

68

Male aged 60 today

79

National life expectancy
At birth, in years, for babies born now, estimated from data over the last few years, since 2012.

X

75

CENTRAL & SOUTH AMERICA

80

CHANGING LIFE EXPECTANCY

These statistics are for the UK but are similar across North America and other developed regions.

year	1900	1910	1920	1930	1940	1950	1960	1970	1980	1990	2000	2010	2020
	51	53	57	61	61	68	72	73	75	76	78	80	82 projected

78 EUROPE

81

81

83

75

72 ASIA

84 HIGHEST

66

65

46 LOWEST

58 AFRICA

62

77 OCEANIA

60

83

Regional life expectancy at birth, years
For babies born now, estimated from data over the last few years, since 2012.

HOW MANY NEW BODIES?

Around the world, 255 new babies are born per minute, that is, more than four every second.
But this is not the global population growth rate because it is balanced by 105 deaths per minute.
So the world gains an extra 150 human bodies per minute, or 210,000 per day—that's the number
of people in a large city. It sounds immense, but it is lower than population growth a few decades ago.

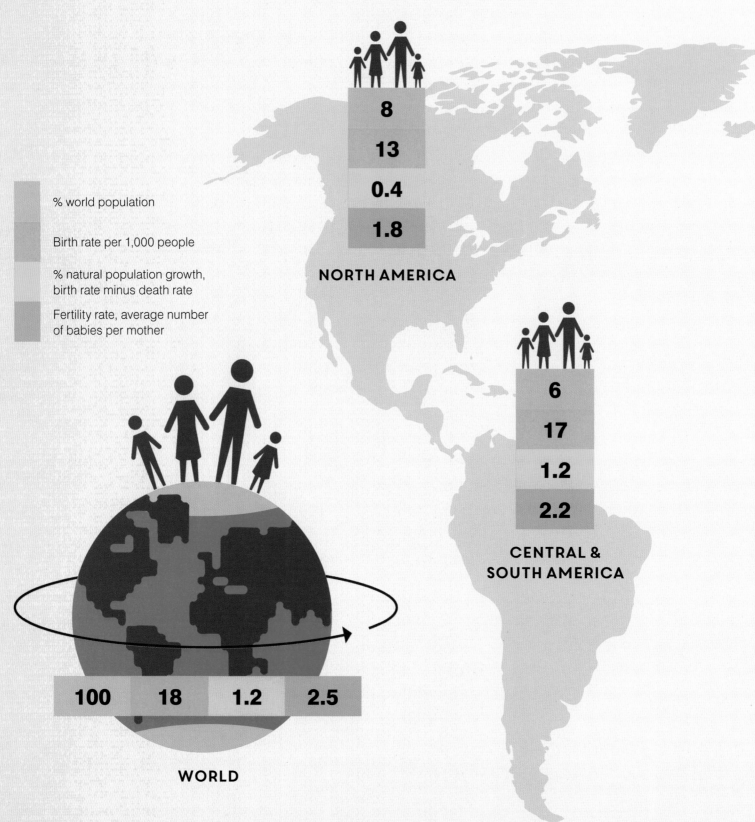

% world population

Birth rate per 1,000 people

% natural population growth,
birth rate minus death rate

Fertility rate, average number
of babies per mother

NORTH AMERICA

8
13
0.4
1.8

**CENTRAL &
SOUTH AMERICA**

6
17
1.2
2.2

WORLD

100
18
1.2
2.5

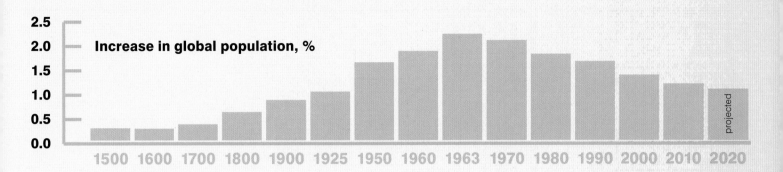

Increase in global population, %

2.5
2.0
1.5
1.0
0.5
0.0

1500 1600 1700 1800 1900 1925 1950 1960 1963 1970 1980 1990 2000 2010 2020

projected

WORLD POPULATION GROWTH RATE, %

The rate at which more bodies arrive on Earth peaked in the early 1960s. In recent years, the number of babies born has remained fairly constant, at about 130–135 million per year. However, the growth rate is falling; as the total rises, these babies form a reducing proportion of that total.

EUROPE

10
12
0
1.6

ASIA

60
22
1.1
2.2

AFRICA

15
38
2.5
4.7

OCEANIA

1
14
1.1
2.4

BABIES AROUND THE WORLD

Birth rates are affected by many factors, from local customs and traditions to religion, economic conditions, and government rulings such as one child per couple.

HOW MANY HUMAN BODIES?

About one person in 16 who has ever lived on Earth, is alive today. Population growth in terms of number of births is steady, although the growth rate falls because they are a smaller proportion of an increasing total. Will an upper limit be reached? Many say we are already living unsustainably, and although human ingenuity for a while may continue to find quick fixes in agriculture and technology, ultimately that will cease.

GLOBAL POPULATION

The number of human bodies in the world at a certain time has,
apart from a couple of hiccups, done nothing but rise—and rise faster.

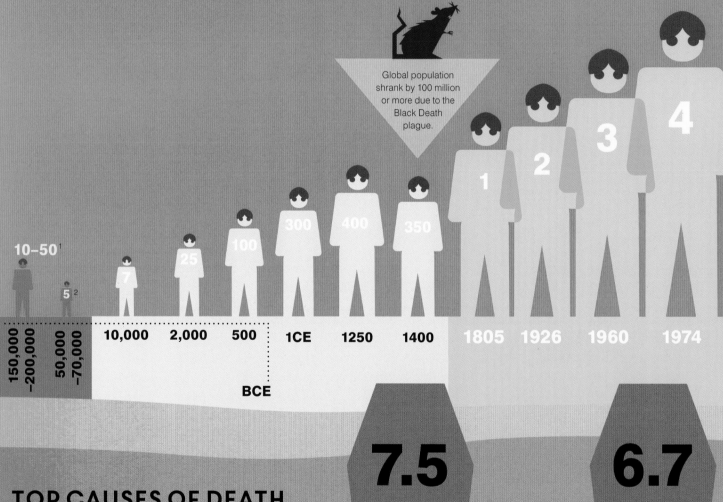

Global population shrank by 100 million or more due to the Black Death plague.

10–50[1]		7	25	100	300	400	350	1	2	3	4
150,000 –200,000	50,000 –70,000	10,000	2,000	500	1CE	1250	1400	1805	1926	1960	1974

5[2]

BCE

TOP CAUSES OF DEATH

in the world (recent years), numbers in millions per year

7.5
Heart disease

6.7
Stroke

1 The "founder" population of our species *Homo sapiens* in East Africa.

2 Genetic, fossil, and climate evidence suggest a "Toba bottleneck," when modern humans (ourselves) and much other life were greatly reduced by the Toba supervolcano eruption in Sumatra.

Thousands

Millions

Billions

5   6   7   8   9   10

1987   1999   2011   2028   2045   2070

3.1

Chronic obstructive pulmonary disease

(emphysema, chronic bronchitis, etc.)

3.1

Lower respiratory infections

(pneumonia, acute bronchitis, etc.)

1.6

Lung and airway cancers

MEDICAL BODY

CAUSES OF ILL HEALTH

According to the World Health Organization: "Health is a state of complete physical, mental, and social wellbeing, and not merely the absence of disease or infirmity." There are many categories of ill health, and their causes often overlap. They can be broken down into the following groupings.

LIFESTYLE & ENVIRONMENT

Lack of exercise contributes especially to
heart disease, stroke, diabetes, cancer, and depression

Smoking tobacco
is a massive contributor to ill health

Environmental causes include
inhaled and contact toxins, infections from poor sanitation, excessive noise, disrupted routines as with shift workers, difficult social conditions

Mental problems include
stress, anxiety, depression

TUMORS & CANCERS

When cells multiply out of control, forming a growth or tumor

Benign tumors are self-contained; malignant or cancerous tumors spread or metastasize

Varied causes and triggers, from carcinogenic chemicals (e.g., tobacco smoke) to radiation (strong sunlight, X-rays), germs, poor diet

IMMUNE SYSTEM & ALLERGIES

The body's immune defense system mistakenly begins to attack its own cells and tissues, known as autoimmunity. Is a component or part of many other conditions.

Examples range from
hay fever and food allergy to diabetes mellitus type 1

INFECTIONS & INFESTATIONS

Caused by germs and parasites

Main groups of germs are
bacteria, viruses, and protozoa

Infectious diseases include
boils and Lyme disease (bacteria), common cold and Ebola (viruses), malaria and sleeping sickness (protozoa)

Infesting parasites include
internal roundworms, tapeworms and flukes, and external fleas, lice, and ticks

INJURY & TRAUMA

May be accidental or deliberate violence.
Can occur anywhere: home, travel, work, leisure.
May result in lasting problems.

DEGENERATIONS

Gradual wearing out and inadequate replacement
at the levels of body cells, parts, and systems

Examples include
osteoarthritis (physical joints), Alzheimer's (nerve cells),
macular degeneration (eye tissues)

NUTRITION

Unhealthy or excessive diet
can contribute to obesity and many illnesses,
and directly cause others

Malnutrition
leads to a host of health problems, such as vitamin deficiency

Lack of hygiene and poor food preparation
may cause food poisoning

Overindulgence
such as too much alcohol, is linked to many
health problems

METABOLISM & PHYSIOLOGY

Problems with the body's myriad chemical processes

Causes range from dietary to genetic and environmental

Include porphyria, acidosis, hemochromatosis

GENES & INHERITANCE

Faulty genes may be inherited or arise in
the body by mutation

Some are inherited in a relatively simple way,
such as sickle cell disease, cystic fibrosis

Many diseases have a less clear genetic component
or tendency, such as breast cancer, schizophrenia

WHAT SEEMS TO BE THE TROUBLE?

Diagnosis (Dx) involves identifying or determining the nature and cause of ill health. All doctors diagnose, but for some it is a specialized field and they become expert diagnosticians. Most medics agree diagnosis is partly a science involving rational consideration of cause and effect, logical selection, and elimination— and partly an art, following suspicions and hunches.

PAIN IN THE ABDOMEN

The body's abdomen is packed with parts and organs. Determining the site of the pain gives clues to its origin and helps toward a diagnosis. Also important is describing the pain: dull or sharp, constant or spasmodic, burning or stabbing, related to diet or movement. The torso is broken down into Quadrants and Regions for better location.

SEEING THE DOCTOR

Japan — 2.3

Germany — 3.9

France — 3.2

Canada — 2.1

Australia — 3.3

UK — 2.8

USA — 2.5

⬤ Number of doctors[1] per 1,000 people

▦ Average number of visits per year to a general practitioner[2]

Left hypochondriac region
- Spleen abscess, enlargement, rupture
- Possible left lung or heart involvement

Umbilical region
- Small intestine, Meckel's diverticulum
- Lymph nodes, lymphoma
- Early appendicitis

Right iliac region
- Appendix, appendicitis
- Large intestine, Crohn's disease
- Ovary cyst, inflammation/infection • Hernia

Epigastric region
- Gullet esophagitis, stricture
- Stomach inflammation (gastritis), ulcer, gas, food toxins
- Pancreas inflammation (pancreatitis)

Right lumbar region
- Right kidney inflammation, infection, (pyelonephritis)
- Ureteric colic (kidney stone trapped in ureter)

Left iliac region
- Large intestine ulcerative colitis, diverticulitis, constipation
- Ovary cyst, inflammation/infection
- Hernia

Right hypochondriac region
- Liver hepatitis, abscess
- Gall bladder inflammation (cholecystitis), gallstones
- Possible right lung or heart involvement

Left lumbar region
- Left kidney inflammation, infection (pyelonephritis)
- Ureteric colic (kidney stone trapped in ureter)

Hypogastric region
- Bladder cystitis, stones, urine retention

1 All officially qualified medical doctors.
2 Officially qualified primary care doctors. Visits tend to be greater in nations with a higher proportion of older people.

MEDICAL INVESTIGATIONS

The discovery of X-rays in 1895 opened up an amazing new world of noninvasive medical imaging. Measuring the heart's electrical pulses, ECG, was developed soon after, in 1901. Today, more than a dozen X-ray and scanning methods diagnose all manner of problems, from a swallowed paperclip to narrowed arteries or tumor growths. And the principle of the ECG has extended to the brain, eye, and other organs.

EEG Electroencephalogram
brain **0.1**

EOG Electrooculogram
eyeball, eye muscles **0.1–1**

ERG Electroretinogram
eye, retina **0.5**

Brain
2,000

Dental
5

Thyroid
4,800

Blood vessels, breast, pelvis
5,000–7,000

Heart
16,000

ECG Electrocardiogram
heart **1–2**

EGG Electrogastrogram
stomach **0.005–0.01**

Mammogram
400

Chest
100

Arm
10

RADIATION EXPOSURE

Almost as soon as X-rays were discovered, their harmful effects became known. In most regions, regulations limit the amount or dose of X-ray radiation that patients receive (and to which staff are regularly exposed).

μSv = microsievert, a measure of radiation dosage

0.1–1 Airport scanner
3,000 Average yearly environmental exposure
20,000–30,000 Full body CT

CT scan

Nuclear scan

X-ray

Coronary angiogram

ELECTRICAL RECORDINGS[1]

Sensor pads or contacts on the body's surface detect the natural, tiny electrical pulses given off by the brain, nerves, heart, and other parts.

Typical voltages mV[2,3]

ULTRASOUND

Sound waves that are too high for our ears to hear are known as ultrasound. They can be adjusted to image different body parts.

1 kHz = kilohertz = 1,000 sound waves per second

10 Upper limit human hearing, older
20 Upper limit human hearing, younger
60 Upper limit dog hearing
200 Upper limit bat hearing
2,500–15,000 Medical ultrasound

Typical wave lengths kHz[1]

MRI

Magnetic resonance imaging uses extremely powerful magnets to align bits of atoms in the body.

Tesla is a unit of magnetic strength, or, more technically, magnetic flux density, one weber per meter squared (one kilogram per second squared per ampere).

0.00005 Earth's natural magnetic field
0.005 Fridge magnet
1 Scrapyard recycling magnet
1.5–3 Typical MRI scanner (humans)
7–15 Powerful MRI scanner (animals)
50+ Scientific research magnets

1 ****_gram is the image, display, or recording produced.
****_graph is the machine that produces it, ****_graphy is the procedure.

2 mV = millivolts = 0.001 or 1/1000th volt.

3 Many of these devices measure voltage change, rather than volts produced.

4 Includes GSR, galvanic skin response. Measures how well the skin conducts electricity, rather than how much electricity it generates, as used in polygraph, or lie detector, devices.

Advances in noninvasive body imaging

X-rays — **1895**

Contrast X-rays — **1896**

Electro-cardiogram — **1901**

Ultrasound — **1949**

C(A)T computerized (axial) tomograph — **1972**

PET positron emission tomography — **1973**

MRI — **1977**

Abdomen pelvis **15,000**

Abdomen, baby **2,500–3,500**

Muscles, superficial tissues **10,000–15,000**

EMG Electromyogram skeletal muscles **0.05–30**

EDA Electrodermal activity[4] skin **n/a**

SURGICAL MEDICINE

Surgery—physically manipulating and altering the body—is no longer limited to "under the knife." Injections, chemicals, lasers, and many other procedures can be involved. Surgical rates differ vastly around the world, and to some extent reflect the health problems and age structure of each nation, as well as the standards of health and medical care. For example, liposuction (fat removal) tends to occur most in rich nations, whereas cataract procedures are relatively more common with aging populations.

HOW MUCH SURGERY?

Proportion of people having one or more surgical procedures in one year.

China	1/40
Argentina	1/30
UK	1/14
Australia	1/9
USA	1/6

Cosmetic procedures

Number of cosmetic procedures per year, including surgical (operations) and nonsurgical (injections, etc.), survey of selected nations.

World total: more than 24 million female and 3 million males

24,000,000

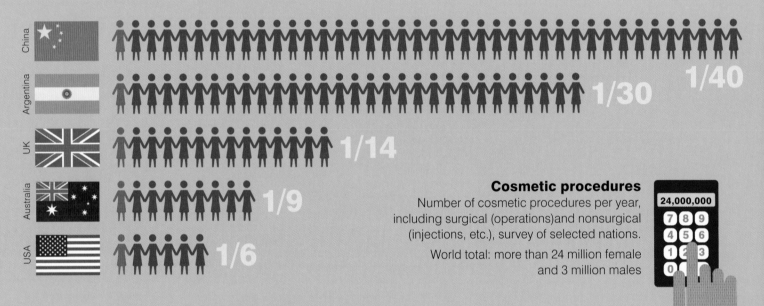

TOP FIVE COSMETIC SURGICAL PROCEDURES % OF TOTAL

15
Eyelids

14
Liposuction

14
Breast augmentation

10
Fat grafting

9
Rhinoplasty (nose)

SURGICAL SPECIALTIES, UK % ALL SURGEONS

29 Trauma, orthopedics

11 other

27 General

Vascular 1

Pediatric 2

Neurosurgery 4

Cardiothoracic 5

Oral, facial 6

6 Urology

9 Otolaryngology (ENT)

CATARACT SURGERY

Cataract removal is the most common life-enhancing and cost-effective surgical procedure in the world. Number of cataract procedures worldwide in millions (estimate):

WHO Vision target

6.5
1990

12
2000

20
2010

32
2020

MEDICAL DRUGS

A drug is virtually anything, apart from normal food and drink, that causes changes in the body. Drugs vary from life-saving antibiotics and "clot busters," to life-threatening abused drugs. Each year the world licenses more drugs and spending increases faster. Better understanding of diseases and genetics, combined with new, quicker, less expensive ways of making custom-made drug compounds are predicted to bring a new era of personalized medicine.

PRESCRIBED DRUGS AND DRUG GROUPS

Seven common prescription drugs worldwide, by generic (chemical) names, group, or therapeutic action.

Hydrocodone
Pain relief (narcotic), cough suppressant (often with acetaminophen, ibuprofen)

Levothyroxine
Thyroid hormone deficiency

Antihypertensive group, ACE inhibitors, calcium blockers
Reduction in high blood pressure, heart conditions

Statin group
Reduction of LDL "bad" cholesterol

Omeprazole group
Acid reflux, digestive ulcers, and bleeding

Metformin
Oral antidiabetic

Azithromycin
(also amoxicillin, similar)
Antibiotics against bacterial diseases

MEDICAL DRUGS THAT CHANGED THE WORLD

1805
MORPHINE
Effective pain relief, still used under controls to prevent addiction

1830s
ASPIRIN
Pain relief, anticlotting, anti-inflammatory; other effects are being discovered

1909
ARSPHENAMINE
(trade name Salvarsan)
Used against syphilis, first example of "magic bullet" chemotherapy

Year	Amount
2008	840
2010	885
2012	935
2014	1,000
2016	1,100 (estimate)
2018	1,250 (estimate)
2020	1,420 (estimate)

BRAND NAME PRESCRIPTION DRUGS

Seven high-sellers worldwide by brand or trade name, with generic or chemical name in brackets, average for recent years (since 2012).

Lipitor (atorvastatin)
Reduction of LDL cholesterol

Nexium (esomeprazole)
Acid reflux, related conditions

Plavix (clopidogrel)
Blood thinner against stroke, heart attack, etc.

Seroquel (quetiapine)
Psychotic conditions such as schizophrenia, bipolar disorder, major depression, related conditions

Singulair (montelukast)
Asthma, allergies, related conditions

Abilify (aripiprazole)
Psychotic conditions such as schizophrenia, bipolar disorder, major depression, related conditions

Advair (salmaterol and fluticasone)
Asthma, COPD, related conditions

1921
INSULIN
First hormone therapy, treatment for diabetes; massively successful

1927
PENICILLIN
First major antibiotic, mass-produced toward the end of World War Two

1951
Antipsychotics such as chlorpromazine, haloperidol helped to control schizophrenia and other mental problems

1962
FUROSEMIDE
For heart conditions, heart failure, high blood pressure (took over from digoxin)

WARS AGAINST CANCERS

There are 200+ kinds of cancers affecting many body parts. Their underlying basis is cells that change, or mutate. They do not follow the usual preprogrammed lifecycle of their kind, but instead start to multiply out of control. They form a growth or tumor that becomes malignant, or cancerous, by spreading to other body parts and growing there, a process called metastasis. Life expectancies for many kinds of cancers have risen in recent decades, some dramatically.

WORLDWIDE

In recent years, **14 million** people per year are diagnosed with cancer, which is 27 per minute.

8 million people per year die from cancer, which is **16 per minute.**

10 MOST COMMON CANCERS WORLDWIDE

10 non-Hodgkin lymphomas (3%) — 85

91 skin melanoma

1 lung[1] (13%) — 17

5 stomach (7%) — 28

8 esophagus (3%)

98 thyroid

6 pancreas

2 breast (12%) — 89

6 liver (6%)

1 Tobacco smoking is the overwhelming cause, estimated to be involved in 80–90% of all cases.

% SURVIVING

Five-year survival rates for selected cancers show the proportion of patients still alive, USA.

99

7 cervix, uterus (4%)

83 uterus

68 cervix

4 prostate (8%)

9 bladder (3%)

95 testis

3 colon, rectum (10%)

65

CANCER SURVIVAL RATES

For all forms of cancer except non-melanoma skin cancer, UK

Year = diagnosed
Five-year survival
Ten-year survival

women
men

%   0   10   20   30   40   50   60   70   80   90   100

1971
1981
1991
2001
2011 (Projected)

CANCER CASES BY NATION

Age-standardized rates of diagnosis, that is, adjusted to a standard age structure, rather than the nation's age profile, to give fairer comparisons. Rate per 100,000 people per year:

338 Denmark
325 France
321 Belgium
318 USA
307 Ireland

284 Germany
273 UK
256 Finland
234 Bulgaria
217 Japan

THE SPARE-PART BODY

Prostheses are artificial or synthetic body parts that hopefully look like, and ideally work like, the real ones. Some are wearable, such as false legs and dentures. Others are surgically inserted or implanted inside the body, such as pacemakers. Transplants are real, living body parts, usually donated by another human. Medical progress and demand have outstripped transplant supply—in most places, for most organs, there are always waiting lists.

1 **c.1,000 BC** Artificial toe (Egyptian mummy)

2 **300 BC** False leg (oldest surviving)

3 **c.700 BC** False teeth (pre-Roman times)

4 **1500s** Hands (mechanical jointed limbs, moving joints)

5 **1790** Dentures (secured full sets)

6 **1901** Blood (blood group transfusions)

7 **1905** Cornea of eye

8 **1940** Artificial hip (much improved 1960s)

9 **1943** Kidney dialysis machine (stationary)

10 **1950s** Artificial shoulder (modular design)

11 **1952** Mechanical heart valve (ball-and-cage/flap designs)

12 **1953** Artificial blood vessel (synthetic materials)

13 **1954** Kidney

14 **1955** Heart valve

15 **1958** Implanted heart pacemaker

16 **1960s** Bionic motorized limb (controlled by signals from stump)

17 **1962** Artificial breast implant (silicone)

18 **1963** Lung

19 **1966** Pancreas

20 **1967** Liver

21 **1967** Heart

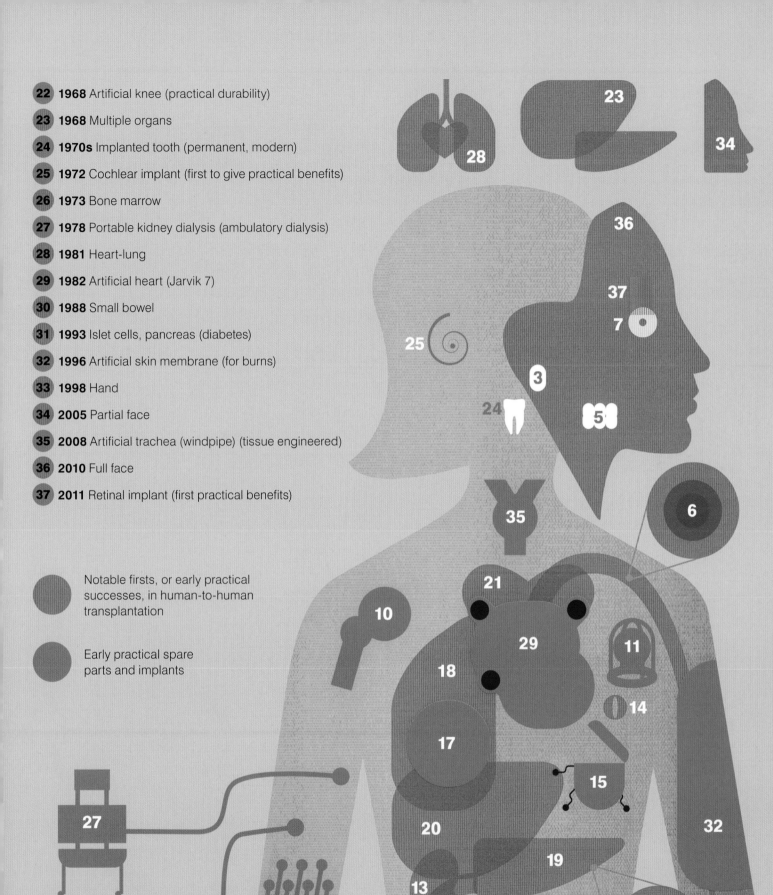

22 **1968** Artificial knee (practical durability)

23 **1968** Multiple organs

24 **1970s** Implanted tooth (permanent, modern)

25 **1972** Cochlear implant (first to give practical benefits)

26 **1973** Bone marrow

27 **1978** Portable kidney dialysis (ambulatory dialysis)

28 **1981** Heart-lung

29 **1982** Artificial heart (Jarvik 7)

30 **1988** Small bowel

31 **1993** Islet cells, pancreas (diabetes)

32 **1996** Artificial skin membrane (for burns)

33 **1998** Hand

34 **2005** Partial face

35 **2008** Artificial trachea (windpipe) (tissue engineered)

36 **2010** Full face

37 **2011** Retinal implant (first practical benefits)

Notable firsts, or early practical successes, in human-to-human transplantation

Early practical spare parts and implants

217

BABIES AND MEDICINE

After one year "trying for a baby," eight out of ten couples (for women, usually up to 45 years) will be expecting. The remaining two may begin to consider advice, and after another year or two, perhaps medical help and assisted fertility or ART, assisted reproductive technology. Of course, for others the opposite outcome is just as desirable: using numerous forms of contraception or birth control.

ASSISTED FERTILITY/REPRODUCTION

Success rates are difficult to determine because some treatments are banking eggs and sperm for future use, and so many factors are involved, such as age, hormonal health, and expertise of practitioners. On average, 30 to 50% of women trying assisted fertility will have a baby in three years.

Fertility drugs
Stimulate or regulate hormonal cycles and ovulation, release of ripe egg from ovary. Equivalent treatments for male involve testosterone.

Gamete intra-fallopian transfer (GIFT)
Early stages similar to IVF. Healthy ripe eggs and sperm placed in oviduct (fallopian tube).

Artificial/donor/intrauterine insemination, AI/DI/IUI
Sperm from the partner, processed for higher fertility, or from a donor, is introduced into the cervix or uterus at ovulation.

Zygote intra-fallopian transfer (ZIFT)
Early stages similar to IVF. Fertilized egg/early embryo (zygote) placed in oviduct (fallopian tube).

Surgery
E.g., to treat narrowed or blocked oviducts (fallopian tubes), fibroids, and other uterine problems in female; testes or tube problems in male.

Surrogacy
Baby is conceived by various methods, e.g., AI, IVF, using the female partner's or donated egg, the male partner's or donated sperm. Another woman, the surrogate, hosts the pregnancy.

BIRTH CONTROL

World estimates for effectiveness of various contraceptive methods in typical everyday use, rather than in theoretical and perfect usage. Figures show number of pregnancies within one year per 100 women.

1 Female hormonal implant
(Fewer than)

70–80
No birth control

2–10
Male condom

1–5 Contraceptive pills (various)

egg harvesting

embryo implanted in uterus

washed sperm

fertilization

egg bathed in washed sperm

embryo

In vitro fertilization, IVF
Ripe eggs (usually obtained by assisted ovulation) and sperm mix outside the female body, leaving fertilization partly to chance. Very early embryos are implanted into the uterus.

Intra-cytoplasmic sperm injection (ICSI)
As for IVF, but one sperm is selected for injection into the egg. Useful for sperm production or health problems.

1–3   Female hormonal injection

Fewer than

1

IUDs (copper, hormonal)

Fewer than

1

Sterilization (female or male)

HOW HEALTHY AND HAPPY?

The past few decades have seen great strides in measuring health, happiness, and wellbeing. This is partly the result of governments and health, social, and medical workers, and many others getting together to decide on evaluating such slippery concepts. Which factors should be included? Which are most important? How are the questions worded? Agreements mean that indicators and measurements can be made, tracked through time, and compared between regions and countries.

BOTTOM 5

TOP 5

Happiness score

7.43

7.56

7.12

7.19

5.82

6.98

FACTORS IN HEALTH AND HAPPINESS

Income and wealth

Job, earnings, employment prospects

Housing, living conditions

Quality of local and wider environment

Health status

Work–life balance

Educational record and satisfaction

Skills achievements

Social life, connections, family and friends

Engagement with civic and government authorities

Personal security

Subjective wellbeing

HAPPIEST DECADES

Surveys finds happiness at different ages in different places.

Australia	11–20	70–79		USA	60–70	21–30	70–80
France	60–70	21–30		UK	50–60	60–70	21–30
Russia	21–30	61–70					

7.59

7.52

7.52

6.87

6.75

6.57

6.33

5.01

3.01

3.99

6.90

5.14

5.99

4.51

3.34

4.25

3.46

2.91

5.48

7.29

2.84

Happiest by nation

The World Happiness Report 2015 (UN based) used indicators such as:

Health
e.g., life expectancy

Economy
e.g., GDP per person

Social support
e.g., friends in a crisis

Corruption
e.g., who's getting a backhander

Generosity
e.g., likelihood of a kind gesture

Ability to make life choices
e.g., a partner of choice rather than custom, when to have a child, when to retire

GLOSSARY

ABSI (a body shape index) A development of BMI that includes waist circumference to take account of body fat distribution; formula for calculating ABSI: waist circumference in meters/(BMI2/3 * √ height in meters).

Alveoli Tiny air sacs in the lungs that yield a vast surface area for gas exchange.

Amygdala Part of brain involved with processing memories, memory consolidation, and with emotions.

Amino acids The building blocks of proteins.

Appendicular skeleton Part of the skeleton consisting of arms and legs.

Artery Blood vessel that takes the blood away from the heart.

Arteriole A small branch of an artery that branches farther into capillaries.

Autoimmunity Immune responses of an organism against its own healthy cells and tissues.

Autonomic nervous system (ANS) Part of the body's nervous system that controls internal functions automatically such as digestion, heartbeat, and breathing. It is made up of the Sympathetic and Parasympathetic nervous systems.

Axial skeleton Part of the skeleton consisting of skull, face, spinal column, and thorax.

Axon Threadlike part of a nerve cell or neuron that transfers a nerve impulse to the dendrites of the next neuron.

Basal ganglia Structures in the brain involved in the control of voluntary movement.

Base pair Refers to a pair of complementary bases that join in strands to form the rungs of the ladderlike DNA.

Biorhythms Recurring cycles in human functioning, such as the sleep/wake patterns and variation in body temperature.

BMI (Body mass index) A formula designed to relate weight to height and therefore possible health implications. The formula is weight in kilograms divided by the square of the height in meters (M÷H2).

Brain stem Links the brain and spinal chord, and contains the centers for basic body processes such as breathing and heartbeat.

Broca's area Part of the brain involved in language, particularly speech.

Capillaries The body's smallest blood vessels.

Cellular respiration Chemical process to generate energy in the cell, producing carbon dioxide.

Cerebrospinal fluid (CSF) Fluid in which brain floats, and which provides physical protection, removes wastes, regulates blood pressure, and supplies some nutrients.

Cerebrum Largest part of brain made up of two cerebral hemispheres, responsible for thought, movement, sensation, and communication.

Cerebellum Lower rear part of the brain concerned with muscle coordination.

Chromosomes Lengths of DNA carrying the body's set of genetic instructions. Humans have 23 pairs of chromosomes.

Circadian Literally, "about one day," referring to the 24-hour activity cycle that the body's daily rhythms follow.

Collagen Structural protein found in connective tissue, providing strength and cushioning.

Corpus callosum The "bridge" in the brain between the left and right cerebral hemispheres.

Corpus luteum Hormone-secreting mass of cells that develops in the ovary after the egg is released.

Cortex The gray matter part of the brain, which is the site of awareness and most conscious thought processes. It is the outer layer of the cerebrum.

Dendrite An extension of a nerve cell along which impulses received from other cells at synapses are transmitted to the cell.

DNA Deoxyribonucleic acid, the body's genetic material, which governs inheritance.

ECG (electrocardiogram) Measurement of the heart's electrical impulses.

EEG (electroencephalogram) Measurement of the electrical activity in the brain.

Embryo The first stage of human development, from after conception until it becomes a fetus at 8 weeks.

Endocrine system Made up of glands that produce and secrete hormones that regulate the activity of cells or organs. Regulate growth, metabolism, sexual development, and many other processes.

Enzymes Substances that act as biological catalysts to bring about a specific reaction, but which remain unchanged at the end.

Extensors Group of muscles that straighten or extend joints.

Extracellular Outside the cell.

Flexors Group of muscles that bend joints.

Follicle Groups of cells found in the ovaries. Secrete hormones that influence the menstrual cycle. Normally one follicle will produce an egg (ovum) in each menstrual cycle.

Fetus A developing human in the second stage, from 8 weeks after conception until birth.

Fornix Part of the brain that contributes to emotional aspects of memory.

Frontal lobe Part of the brain involved in emotional function, important cognitive functions such as problem solving, short-term memory, and the combining of memory elements into conscious awareness.

Gamete Sex cell, which has half the number of chromosomes of an ordinary cell. Male gamete is sperm; female gamete is the ovum or egg.

Ganglion cells Neurons that relay information from the retina to the brain via the optic nerve.

Gene Short section of DNA carrying the genetic instruction for a single inherited property. Human DNA contains thousands of genes that control how the body and all its parts develop, work, maintain, and repair themselves.

Glial cells Specialized "glue" cells that support nerve cells and hold them in place.

Hemoglobin Red-colored chemical in blood cells that carries oxygen around the body.

Hippocampus Part of the brain involved in memory consolidation and spatial memory.

Hormones The body's control chemicals produced by the endocrine system.

Hypothalamus Part of brain involved in bodily expression of emotions.

Integumentary system Body system concerned with skin, hair, nails, and sweat glands for protection, temperature control, and waste removal.

Interstitial Around cells.

Intracellular Inside the cell.

Keratin Type of fibrous protein found in hair and nails.

Limbic system Body system that contributes to feelings, moods, and emotions.

Lymphatic system System for draining general body fluids, collecting waste, and repairing and defending the body.

Malignant Altered cells tending to grow out of control and spread rapidly; may cause death.

Medulla oblongata Part of the underbrain involved in many automatic (autonomic or involuntary) processes, actions, and reflexes, including heart rate, breathing rate, blood pressure, and digestive activity.

Meiosis The kind of cell division that occurs to make eggs and sperm. The number of chromosomes in the resulting cells is halved.

Meninges Three protective layers around the brain.

Metabolism Term to describe the chemical reactions, changes, and processes (many of them linked and interdependent) occurring in every cell of the body.

Metastasize/Metastasis Spread of cancer from one part of the body to another.

Mid brain Part of the brain concerned with automatic body maintenance.

Mitochondria Structures in the cytoplasm of cells where energy is produced.

Mitosis Process of asexual cell division that results in two identical cells.

MRI (Magnetic resonance imaging) A diagnostic technique that produces images of the body's soft tissue and bone using strong magnetic fields and radio waves.

Myelin sheath Fatty protective covering of axons of nerves. It increases the speed a nerve impulse can travel along an axon.

Neurons Nerves cells, the basic cells of the nervous system.

Neurotransmitter Chemical released from a nerve cell, which transmits nerve impulses across a synapse.

Nucleosome Basic unit of DNA packaging; a "bead" on the necklace of DNA.

Olfaction To do with smell. Its control center in the brain is the olfactory bulb.

Organelles Specialized structures found in a cell, such as the nucleus and mitochondria.

Parasympathetic autonomic nervous system (PANS) Part of the autonomic nervous system, whose function is to conserve the body's energy by, for example, slowing the heart rate and breathing.

Parietal Lobe in the brain coordinating sensory information.

Pennation angle Angle of muscle fiber, which has implications for how much force is transmitted/how muscle and skeleton work together.

Peristalsis Involuntary muscular waves along the digestive tract that facilitate moving of food.

Peripheral nervous system Refers to all the nerves in the body, excluding the brain and spinal cord.

Pineal gland Gland found in the brain that produces the hormone melatonin, which regulates sleep–wake patterns.

Pituitary gland Master gland of the hormone system located just below the brain.

Pons The link between the lower and higher parts of the brain. Basic processes such as swallowing and urination, sleep and dreams are controlled here.

Proprioception The knowing or being aware of the positions, postures, and movements of body parts.

Prostheses Artificial or synthetic body parts.

Puberty Stage of development when the sexual organs and the body become mature.

RNA Ribonucleic acid, which acts as a messenger between DNA and protein-forming systems of a cell.

Somatosensory cortex The touch centers of the brain.

Sympathetic autonomic nervous system (SANS) Prepares the body for intense physical activity—the fight-or-flight responses, such as increasing heart and breathing rates, so that the body can respond more effectively.

Synapse The junction between nerve cells, which is a small gap.

Thymus A specialized lymph gland in the neck and thorax, which produces specialized white blood cells to fight disease.

Thalamus Twinned egg-shaped masses in the brain which act as gatekeeper to the cortex and conscious mind.

Thyroid gland Found in the neck and regulates the metabolism and speed of body processes.

Vein Blood vessel that carries blood toward the heart.

Venule A small branch of a vein collecting blood from the capillaries.

Vestibular system General name of the inner-ear structures relating to balance.

Villi Threadlike hairs found in on and around cells that increase the surface area without increasing the volume.

Wernicke's area Part of the brain involved in language, particularly the comprehension of speech and the written word.

Zona Thick membrane around the ovum which prevents multiple sperm from penetrating it.

Zygote The first cell of a new individual following fertilization.

Quarto is the authority on a wide range of topics. Quarto educates, entertains, and enriches the lives of our readers—enthusiasts and lovers of hands-on living. www.QuartoKnows.com

First published 2016 by
Aurum Press Limited, an imprint of The Quarto Group
The Old Brewery, 6 Blundell Street,
London, N7 9BH

This new edition first published in 2019

Illustrations by Andrew Baker
Art Direction and layout by JenniferRoseDesign.co.uk
Text copyright © 2016 Steve Parker
The moral right of Steve Parker to be identified as the author of this work has
been asserted by him in accordance with the Copyright, Designs and Patents Act 1988.

A catalogue record for this book is available from the British Library.

ISBN 978 1 78131 850 8

10 9 8 7 6 5 4 3 2 1

Printed China